GOING HOME:

A NETWORKING
SURVIVAL GUIDE

William H. Bishop

In Going Home, former Chief Petty Officer Bishop outlines a step-by-step process for successfully transitioning that is applicable to all service members. He teaches the reader how to translate military jargon into coherent data to list on a resume. Most importantly, he teaches the reader the importance of networking, a vital skill in today's global economy.

—Admiral Vern Clark, US Navy (ret.), former Chief of
Naval Operations

Bill Bishop's Going Home is a remarkably insightful and timely guide to military veterans transitioning to civilian life. Filled with down-to-earth, practical advice from an outstanding leader, this book will be extremely useful in helping all veterans preparing the next stage of their lives.

—Bill George, Professor, Harvard Business School,
former Chair & CEO of Medtronic,
and author of *True North*

Bishop's "Going Home" is a quintessential tool for anyone seeking to make a career transition. This practical and insightful guide provides practical advice to anyone navigating through these changes. William's voice lends a timely yet timeless message related to the skills needed to network in today's social world.

—Philip A Foster, CEO, Maximum Change, Inc.

In my over two decades of consulting in the private and defense sectors, this is the first complete book of its kind for anyone considering a transition from military service to civilian life. A must-have for every service member.

—Dr. Toks Idowu, Chairman and C.E.O. of the LCI Cooper Group.

Going Home is chocked full of relevant and practical information on how to step confidently from the battlefield into the civilian arena. Bishop's book is a valuable addition to the bookshelf whether you're retiring after a successful military career or moving on after your first tour of duty. A definite read before you start the job search, a serious reread before an interview and a reference you'll return to over and over as your new career develops. I haven't read better!

—June Forte, President, Virginia Writers Club

This book, "Going Home" looks at networking from a fresh perspective, nothing like you ever considered. Bishop's insights provide well-rounded insight into how networking is done and how transitioning can occur successfully—from a practical perspective undergirded with solid academic insights. The text provides the reader with good solid sugges-

*tions on how to make transitions while being guided in a way
that is both deliberate and smart.*

—Kathleen Patterson, Ph.D., Associate Professor,

Regent University

This book is dedicated first to God, who is the Alpha and Omega, the beginning and end, the Creator of all things good, my Savior. Second, it is dedicated to my wife, Barbara, who is my greatest champion and very best friend without whom I would be nothing. Third, it is dedicated to those who know what it means to be away from home for prolonged periods in service to their country.

CONTENTS

FOREWORD

Congratulations! The fact that you have this book in your hand means you have taken the first step to building that safety net we call our networks and success-fully making the transition to civilian life.

The concept of changing a career can be daunting. Add to it the transition from military to civilian life and the stress is exponentially increased. *Going Home* is the perfect antidote for that stress. Author and former US Navy Chief Petty Officer William Bishop has written a book about this transition, which he has personally experienced, endured, and prevailed.

This book is organized in a logical progression that focuses both on how to prepare for your transition as well as what to do. Bill does what many people of integrity do: he tells the truth even when it's not pretty and also provides a viable plan for you to review and replicate. Most of us know we must have a support team and build a network. William Bishop provides a practical guide for how to do it.

For some, the concept of networking is alien, uncomfortable, and often seems to be unnatural and maybe even inauthentic. Bill Bishop provides the guideline, punctuated with relevant stories and examples that underscore his points in this easy-to-read, ready-to-implement book that resonates with those of us who have to assess our skills and experiences and transfer them to a new career.

Going Home is your in-print mentor.

Susan RoAne
Keynote speaker and author of *How to Work a Room*
and *The Secrets of Savvy Networking*

INTRODUCTION

My story is not unlike a lot of service members'. I spent a little over thirteen years in the navy before being medically discharged. I had a promising career until a medical condition landed me on limited duty (LIMDU, in navy parlance). Within a relatively short time, I learned that my naval career would likely be coming to an end. The navy was downsizing, and anyone on limited duty stood a good chance of going home if they weren't curable: I wasn't. I had a degenerative condition that would only get worse with time and would need to be managed for the rest of my life, which meant my navy days were numbered.

That was quite a sobering thought, especially with the economic uncertainty the country was experiencing at the time. I had been to TAP (transition assistance program) several years before when I was dubious about my career prospects, but TAP alone wasn't the answer. TAP provided some great guidance and general information, but I soon realized that more was required if I was going to land a rewarding job in a new line of work.

I had recently completed my MBA at Regent University. My long-term goal was to pursue a doctorate so that I could teach at the college level. That degree was going to take several years to complete, and I only had a short time before circumstances came crashing down around me. I needed to form a plan that would ensure I found a good job that allowed me to provide for my family and maintain our current lifestyle.

The first, and perhaps best, thing I did was contact Dave Boisselle, Director of Military Affairs at Regent University. Although I didn't know it at the time, this single action would have a cascading effect on my life. It opened my eyes to the value of networking and put me on track to develop a multitude of relationships that were mutually beneficial. Dave helped me with my resume and provided exceptional career guidance. We formed an immediate rapport and thus began a great friendship. Over the next several months, Dave guided me and advised me on associations to join, seminars to attend, and introduced me to the right people. I learned a lot from him. Perhaps the critical thing I learned from him, though, was the value of networking.

We've all networked in the military. If we didn't, things wouldn't get done. Actually, they would, but they would just take longer. Although we all did it, we never called it "networking." We called it a "hook up." Well, networking is very much like a hook up; it's just applied a little differently in the civilian world, and it's even more vital there than it is in the military. "In its simplest form, networking is a reciprocal process in which you share ideas, leads, information, advice, brainstorming, laughter ... and sometimes tickets to a ball game," says author John Maxwell.[1] Essentially, networking is getting to know people in various capacities and circles of influence. It is about forming relationships. Networking provides the means; relationships provide the opportunity.

Building a network is a lot like constructing a spider web, and it functions in a similar manner. You start by weaving a single strand of a web, the first step of the journey, and connect it to the securest structure (person) you can find. In my case, it was Dave. Then you continue to add strands (people) who know other people (more strands) until you have the form of an actual web. It may begin as a small web, but it is nevertheless a web. As I will discuss in the following chapters, you solidify that web before you continue to add to it, and you check it regularly for flies (people). The smallest web can collect the largest of flies, so never concern yourself about your network's size. It's the strength that counts!

What I mean by the strength is how well connected the people in your network are. Initially, my network consisted of Dave Boisselle. Dave is very well connected in the military realm, academic arena, and the community. After I met Dave, I connected with a gentleman who was well established in his local community. He belonged to a Rotary Club and was a prominent volunteer. Another member of my network was connected with the military and veterans' network. These three people bolstered my network and made it extremely strong.

One thing about networking that I never realized until I started doing it is that networking is really about leadership. In his *New York Times* best seller *The 21 Irrefutable Laws of Leadership*, John Maxwell states, "Leadership is influence ... nothing more, nothing less."[2] Well, networking is also about influence. When you network with others, you engage with them in a way that can influence them (and they can influence you as well) and their decision making, initially, perhaps, to hire you. However, after you have networked for a while, you'll soon realize how much you have to offer others. "The very first aspect to influencing your personal network is to first establish a solid trusting relationship between you and everyone you know in your network. By doing so it gives you a very influential role in the lives of those you know in the network themselves," states Scott Bradley.[3] And, I concluded, if Maxwell is correct about leadership and influence—and I believe he is—then networking is also about leadership.

Now, you may not be providing direct leadership in this application in the sense you are leading someone to a particular conclusion or place in his or her life. What you are really doing is providing indirect leadership, which is nothing more than yielding to them—what some call *followership*. There's a saying that to be a good leader you need to be a good follower, which is where we get the term *followership*.

Lieutenant Colonel Sharon Latour notes, "Without follow-ership, a leader at any level will fail to produce effective institutions."[4] The principal point of this perspective is that by following others and *serving them* you can also lead them and thus influence them. This is the heart of networking and is the basis of servant leadership.

As Larry Spears, former president and CEO for the Greenleaf Center for Servant Leadership, notes, "A particular strength of servant-leadership is that it encourages everyone to actively seek opportunities to both serve and lead others, thereby setting up the potential for raising the quality of life throughout society."[5] Although I didn't know it at the time, I eventually realized that networking is truly about servant leadership. And the best networkers I met were the ones who served others by making helpful suggestions, connecting people, or getting personally involved with others and form-ing meaningful relationships.

So with the concept that networking is about leader-ship in mind, I set out on my networking journey to find a good job in a flailing economy, which was no small task. My experience and ability to network with the right people not only helped me start my own company, but provided me with the opportunity to teach others how to network to add value to their lives and reciprocate on a large scale. I didn't follow any formula or use any special techniques. I merely applied the principles that follow. They were learned by trial and error, lectures from professionals, books, seminars, and most of all practice. They take time, but they work. I hope you find them to be of benefit during your transition from the military to the civilian workforce.

Acknowledgments

I would like to thank everyone who made this book possible. First and foremost, I would like to thank my friend Dave Boisselle for inspiring me to tell my story and develop it into something that others could use and for taking the time to painstakingly edit it. A simple e-mail with a suggestion to capture my story was the impetus for the contents of the following pages. At the time I began writing it, I never imagined it would take me on a journey of its own. Compiling my story was only the beginning. New twists and turns were had along the way as I met with military veterans and learned how networking played a pivotal role in their lives.

Additionally, I would to thank Lieutenant Commander Bart Denny, my former department head from the USS *Deyo* (DD-989), one of the greatest ships that ever sailed. Bart was a mentor during my early days in the navy, and he later became a good friend and confidant. I can always rely on him for frank and sound advice as well as constructive criticism. These are the traits that make him such an effective leader and are what make him such a great friend today.

Included among those who deserve thanks is Philip Foster. Philip and I met through Regent University's Doctor of Strategic Leadership program. Philip provided valuable suggestions that greatly contributed to the overall flow and organization of the manuscript. His years of life-coaching experience were immeasurably beneficial in the development of the goal-setting method discussed in chapter one.

I want to recognize and thank the veterans who not only shared their experience and wisdom with me, but also served their country honorably in its defense: Bart Denny, Kenisha Thompson, Matthew Klym, Riley Hensley, and A. J. Magnan.

I want to especially thank Susan RoAne, author of *How to Work a Room*, who practices what she preaches. We met at a Regent University Executive Leadership Series luncheon and spoke briefly afterward. I wanted to share my system of tracking people's business cards by taping them to a sheet in a Moleskine notebook with her, so I e-mailed her. I never expected to get a response directly from her and was quite pleased when I did. After I started writing this book, I contacted her again for input. After all, she's the expert! She was extremely gracious and allowed me to use excerpts from essays she had written. Her willingness to assist and support me is a testimony to her character and the quality of what she does. Thank you, Susan! You are truly a networker's networker.

Last but not least, I want to thank Dr. Bramwell Osula for his meticulous review and accompanying suggestions. His comments proved that good writing is all in the details!

CHAPTER ONE

NEW BEGINNINGS: SETTING GOALS AND TAKING STOCK

~The SMART Method~

P erhaps you chose to leave the armed forces and pursue another line of work or maybe you are the victim of government or corporate downsizing. In either case, you have entered a new chapter of your life. It can be an exciting chapter; it can be a scary chapter. It's a time filled with apprehension, fear, stress, and anxiety. You will experience many highs and many lows when you first exit the military. One way to establish balance during this time is to set goals. Goal setting is a means to determine where you want to go and when you have arrived there. It is a means of measuring the success of your plan (covered in chapter two).

Much like a career in the corporate world, you joined the military for a reason. Perhaps it was to get an education, see the world, take an alternate route to college, or a desire to serve your country. Whatever the case, you entered the military with a goal, so exiting should be no different. There are many ways to set goals for yourself. One popular and successful way is the SMART method. It stipulates goals should be specific, measurable, actionable, realistic, and timed.

- *Specific.* Broadly defined goals are difficult to measure, and because they are difficult to measure, many people fail to achieve their goals. In reality, they never really had a good idea of what they wanted to achieve. It's analogous to someone saying, "I want to get in shape." What does that mean? To some, getting in shape might mean attaining the goal of running a mile in ten minutes. Someone else might define it as running a marathon in less than three hours. Specificity is the cornerstone of goal setting. The more specific the goal, the easier it is to measure and achieve.
- *Measurable.* Goals must be measurable over time. You might want to complete a college degree or obtain a particular certification. These things take time, but they can take even longer if you don't keep track of them from the beginning. For example, if

you want to complete a college degree, do you have a time frame in mind? If so, have you taken the time to measure how many credits you will need to take each semester so you reach your goal on time? Time is the most precious commodity in the world, and its effective management is critical to achieving goals.

- *Actionable.* Goals are desires that are transformed into action. They are not dormant ideas left on the proverbial drawing board. Establishing a goal is a prelude to action. It demands movement, momentum, and initiative! Goals require you to do something. They are predicated on future events—weekly trips to the gym, regular deposits in a savings account, a certain number of pages read each night, and the like. Your goals require action. Left idle, they will become the foundation of wishful thinking.

- *Realistic.* Goals are a great way to incite us to action to fulfill our dreams. However, if our goals are not realistic, we are unlikely to achieve them, and thus we become discouraged. So, what is a realistic goal? Well, a realistic goal is one that can be achieved with a proper amount of effort and planning commensurate with an individual's abilities and resources. Essentially, your goal has to be something you have the time, money, and ability to achieve. For example, your goal might be to go to law school. Okay, that's doable. First, you need a bachelor's degree from an accredited university. Second, you need to do well on the Law School Admission Test (LSAT). There are many LSAT prep books and courses available to assist you. Third, you need the money to pay for law school. Fourth, you need the time. Most law schools are full-time, so that's three years of school. Fifth, you need the ability to do the academic work required. If you have these things in place, or you can put them in place, then attending law school is a realistic goal.

- *Timed.* Timed goals are similar to measured goals. The difference, though, is that one is measured in units other than time. For example, a goal of losing weight would be *measured* in pounds, but it would be *timed* by setting a date for realistic weight loss: for example, ten pounds in one month. The reason a goal needs to be timed is that, as with measurement, if you have no way to assess your progress, you are likely to lose focus, get off track, and become discouraged. If that happens, any goal you have will typically be abandoned in the pile of good intentions.

Establishing your goals is the critical first step of the process to find a decent job, change careers, or start your own company. Your goals will set the tone for your networking journey and serve as a road map. They will be your starting point, so take some time, use the SMART method, and write down your goals. Assess them honestly and discuss them with those to whom you are closest—a spouse, family member, colleague, or close friend. Solicit their input. What you decide you would like to do will determine your actions and how you assess your abilities as they relate to networking. Ask yourself the following questions to assess your goals:

- Is my goal specific?
- Can it be measured? If so, how?
- What action is required?
- Is it realistic?
- What is my time frame for accomplishing this goal?

Darren Shearer highlights five tips for setting goals:

1. *Set goals for every aspect of your life.* "While it is important to focus on what we are good at, it is critical to ensure that we live well-balanced lives."
2. *Set daily, monthly, and long-term goals.* "Every goal should be measurable. So when you set goals, make sure that you specify the date, month, or year by which you want to achieve that goal."
3. *Write down or type out your goals.* "Whether it is a daily 'to-do' list or goals, or a long-term list of lifetime goals, they should be written down or typed out."

4. *Count the cost of each goal.* "By counting the cost of [your] goals, [you] will discover what [your] values truly are."

5. *Constantly visualize your goals.* "Every goal must first be visualized before you will be able to whole-heartedly pursue it."[6]

~Take Stock~

Before you can build your network, start looking for a job, or launch your own business, you must honestly evaluate who you are, where you have been, and what you can realistically do in the civilian job market. What does all of your experience mean? How does it relate to a civilian job, a new career, or your own business? What kind of job are you best suited for? What kind of career would you enjoy? What type of business would you like to establish? Well, first things first. Get organized! Preparing information for your resume is a lot like completing a research paper; preparing a special programs package, such as an instructor, recruiter, or special warfare package; or submitting a selection board package. You have to gather your source data and organize it into a cohesive format.

Compile your performance evaluations, personal awards, military training jacket, experience transcript, and other relevant documentation. Read them several times and highlight the pertinent information. There is a plethora of information in them. You want to separate the stuff from the fluff because that is what is going on your resume, so be sure to take notes. Apply the same keen eye you were taught to use by your superiors when reviewing your performance evaluations. Look for the verbs and nouns that tell *what* you actually did. How *well* you did it will come later. The most important things to extract are (1) what you did, (2) its impact, and (3) the result. Remember the phrase "What impact resulted?" (WIR). Good performance evaluations, both military and civilian, are written this way, so in most cases it should not be too difficult. This exercise may come in handy later during job interviews, which often focus on the same type of information. Interviewers typically look for the situation, task, action, and result (STAR).

Pull the information from your service and employment records and organize it. You can do this by command, job, job title, rank, navy enlisted classification (NEC), military occupational specialty (MOS), or whatever category best suits your job in the military or corporate world. Now, after organizing and reading all of your information, ask yourself, what picture does it paint? Would you be suited as a construction worker (blue collar) or are you the administrative type (white collar)? Is law enforcement a possibility or would hotel management be a better fit? Honestly critique your experience because employers will. As Popeye the Sailor says, "I am what I am." And you are what you are.

A quick way to get a snapshot of who you are according to your evaluations is to read the opening and closing statements. Sure the information in between, sometimes in bullet format, gives some really specific details about what you have done and how well you did it, but the opening and closing statements tell a discerning reader what really needs to be known. For example, does your opening statement indicate you are in the top echelon of your peer group in the organization, for example, number one out of twenty technicians; number three out of forty administrators; or that you are performing the job of the next higher rank or pay grade? What about the closing statement and promotion recommendation? Are you strongly recommended for early promotion and enhanced career assignment? These are indications that you were highly proficient and effective at your job and should help you in the equivalent civilian job.

In *Education & Training,* Fallows and Steven noted,

Today's challenging economic situation means that it is no longer sufficient for a new graduate to have knowledge of an academic subject; increasingly it is necessary for students to gain those skills which will enhance their prospects of employment. Employability skills include the following abilities: the retrieval and handling of information; communication and presentation; planning and problem solving; and social development and interaction.[7]

Look for consistency, increased job responsibility, and proficiency. Most job announcements are targeted at people with a variety of specific competencies as they pertain to a specific job. Organizing your opening and closing statements will give you a quick indication as to whether you are suited for a particular job in a general sense. If a job looks like a match, it's time to start comparing your experience to the job requirements. This is where WIR comes into play.

What impact resulted is the extracted information from your performance appraisals that translates into knowledge, skills, and abilities. This is what potential employers look for in a candidate. It tells them what you can *do* for them, what you bring to the table. More importantly, it gives them a reason to hire you. It is also the criteria you will need to use if you decide to go into business for yourself. After all, you must determine what it is you have to *offer* customers in order to venture out on your own.

Begin with *what* (W) you did. Examples of words that fit in this category are managed, supervised, implemented, orchestrated, conducted, organized, and so on. These are action words that tell what you did. After you jot them down, add the component item to them: for example, *managed* three work centers, *supervised* ten subordinates, *implemented* a new safety policy, *orchestrated* a command program, *conducted* training, *organized* a command event, and so on. Pull this information from your evaluations and simplify it as above.

Now look at how effective *what* you did was—its *impact* (I). This is where a lot of fluff can be found in evaluations. As a chief petty officer, I have reviewed many performance evaluations. To my chagrin, I have seen too much empty hyperbole used in this area, often in an attempt to boost a sailor's appeal for advancement. Though this might sometimes be effective in the navy—and that's certainly debatable—it won't fly in the civilian world. For example, "Sailor Y managed three work centers flawlessly and meticulously, which improved the morale of the division and increased productivity while decreasing equipment downtime." Sounds good, right? Wrong! It's fluff. While the owner of this evaluation might feel good about himself, it says nothing about the real *impact* of what he did. Stating the real impact answers questions a reader might ask: How much was productivity increased (dollars, percentage, etc.)? How much equipment downtime was there to begin with, and how much was it decreased (days, weeks, months, etc.)?

Develop a critical eye when reading your evaluations, particularly as you assess the impact of what you did. Apply the same techniques you were taught by your mentors and leaders as you review your evaluations. Look for factual data, not just descriptive adjectives. For example, "Sailor Y managed three work centers with a combined budget of over $1 million dollars and ensured 100 percent accuracy in parts accountability, which greatly improved the morale of twenty-three divisional members by affording them more time off due to a 20 percent reduction in equipment downtime." See the difference? The impact should be specific because that is what you are going to apply to a job announcement.

Finally, identify the *results* (R) of your actions. In other words, how did *what* you did benefit others? This is very similar to the impact, yet it is decidedly different because it relates to *people*. You may have saved your work center thousands of dollars in parts (impact), but the *result* was a commendation from the commanding officer. You might have managed a large budget without discrepancy (impact), but the *result* was special liberty for your division. Remember, results always relate to people. Even if what you did is related to the command, the command is composed of people. Find the people who benefited from your actions, and you will see the results.

Figure 1.1. A WIR chart.

W	I	R
Managed	Reduced cost	Commendation
Supervised	Improved morale	Special liberty
Implemented	Increased Operability	
Orchestrated		
Conducted		
Organized		

When you start using this process, simply write W I R across the top of a blank page, spacing the letters out equally. Divide each into a separate column and list the information appropriately under each category (Figure 1.1). Try to use only a few key words under each as shown in the example. This is a valuable exercise that will allow you to create a snapshot of who you are and what you have to offer a civilian company. And it will provide you with a quick reference for comparison to a job announcement. In the same way you look at your evaluations for key words, you can apply the same technique to a job announcement and list the critical qualifications necessary (Figure 1.2).

Figure 1.2. A job announcement. Key words are in bold.

This position is responsible for **managing** the .... This position will **assist** in the development and coordination of ... **work** closely with applicants from the point of application ... **acquire** and maintain a knowledge ... and **travel** as assigned to college fairs, seminars, church meetings, etc.

As you review a job announcement, look for *what* the job requires—knowledge, skills, and abilities—and think about your WIR. These key words are in bold type in Figure 1.2. List these on a separate WIR chart. Just as with your evaluations, the component items follow. Now compare the two. Do the W columns reflect similar skills and abilities? If so, how do the component items relate to those from your evaluations? This is the place to begin as you review job announcements. To be competitive for a job, your knowledge, skills, and abilities (commonly referred to as KSA) should match that of the job by 80 percent or more, and your experience should be commensurate.

The *New York Times* reported a new technique for assessing a candidate's compatibility with a position:

> Candidates arrive at screening interviews only to meet a computer. They spend about half an hour at a screen, answering software-generated questions pertaining to the job they're after. The computer gathers information about the person's knowledge, background, skills and abilities, and then sends it along to the hiring manager. Using technology this way may eliminate the need for a resume, but it adds a new hurdle for candidates to clear before winning a face-to-face interview—and a job.[8]

Ensuring your KSAs match those of a job announcement is vital to obtaining an interview. Carefully examine the items you list under W. Are these terms synonymous with the knowledge required in a job announcement? Do the impacts that resulted translate into skills and abilities? Use a separate chart to compare the two lists

Okay, you're saying you don't want to do the same thing you did in the military or in your previous position; you want a fresh start. That involves something more, and we'll cover that in the next few chapters. For now, you need to honestly assess your experience. Do this early and often. There's an old saying about saving for retirement: The best time to start saving is yesterday. The second-best time is today. The same is true for assessing your professional experience. If you think you are going to leave the military service, be discharged for any reason, or are planning to change careers, assess yourself. In fact, assess yourself throughout your career. It's good preparation for the future. And if you plan to stay for twenty years or more or to maintain your career in a given field and have an employment goal for retirement or life after your current career, assessment is critical to developing a plan to get there.

Assess yourself honestly. You'll hardly pick up everything with one assessment, so go over your record several times, reread your awards, and go through your service record, SMART transcript, and training jacket. Review your education and certifications. Look for qualifications, schools, and training that have relevance in the corporate world or might have relevance in a desired career field. To find out what might have relevance, look at job listings. Don't just look at the ones that appeal to you as far as location and salary or the ones that tickle your fancy. Look at the ones that match your qualifications. How do you match up?

Now step back and throw the first punch—at yourself! If you don't critique your record honestly, you'll be job hunting for a long time, so don't hold back. Your particular job in the military might not translate into much in the civilian world. If it doesn't, so be it. Tearing away the flesh from the bone is the only way you are going to know what you really have to offer an employer, so don't kid yourself and believe the military press. There are many superstars in the military and corporate America who received good evaluations and numerous awards and were the go-to person. But the game is played differently in the global economy, so don't expect those things to land you a great job. Don't fear, though; you still have some golden nuggets that can be salvaged. And gold, even in small quantities, is valuable.

Once you've taken stock, be prepared to be surprised. Military experience doesn't always transfer well into the civilian world, but that doesn't mean it doesn't transfer at all. Of critical importance is being able to translate your military experience into civilian language. This is a common obstacle for everyone who transitions from the military. In fact, it is also an impediment to seasoned corporate workers who are seeking to advance their careers, so don't fret. Even though you might have been highly qualified in the military, no one in the civilian world may care or appreciate the things you did because they don't understand their significance. That's okay; there are gems in your service record that can be polished. For example, being qualified to drive a ship at sea might not mean a whole lot to someone at a financial advisory firm. However, maintaining several million dollars' worth of government property without incident or loss demonstrates your level of competence and responsibility. Get the idea?

If you ran a division of ten people and were responsible for the maintenance and upkeep of a weapon system, that might fall under your ability to supervise, lead, and manage. Or you might have maintained several million dollars in repair parts or managed several hundred service records. It's all in how you read it. More importantly, it's all in how you apply it to the job you want. So keep that in mind as you compare the two. Those few golden nuggets may be just enough to get your resume noticed by an employer, and that might lead to an interview and perhaps a job!

~Networking Basics~

Taking stock of your experience arms you for the task at hand: networking. The term *networking* can mean a lot of things to different people. In our case, it simply means incorporating others' spheres of influence with yours. Susan RoAne, the Mingling Maven, observes, "We all have networks. We were born into them, went to school with them, were in after-school activities and clubs, attended camps, played sports, went to religious school, worked, volunteered for charity and lived in neighborhoods with other people. We still do."[9] We call them relationships, or friendships. Well, networking is the same thing, only it involves making new friends and building new relationships with people who can influence our employment prospects and career potential. Think of a network as a set of concentric circles of influence (Figure 1.3). Your goal is to add more people to your circles of influence, connect all of the circles of influence to each other, and thus expand your network.

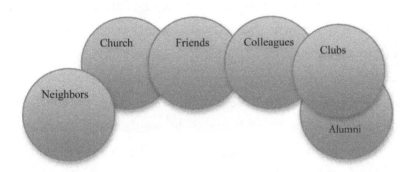

Figure 1.3. A network is connected circles of influence.

You might think the concept of networking sounds a little like using people. Professors Herminia Ibarra and Mark Hunter of Insead in Fontainebleau, France concluded in their article *How Leaders Create and Use Networks*,

Many find networking insincere or manipulative—at best, an elegant way of using people. Not surprisingly, for every [person] who instinctively constructs and maintains a useful network, [there are] several who struggle to overcome this innate resistance. Yet the alternative to networking is to fail—either in reaching for a leadership position or in succeeding at it.[10]

Networking, though, is really about harnessing the power of the relationship. We do it all the time. Have you ever asked your friend who owns a truck to help you move? Has your best friend asked you to housesit while she is on vacation? That is harnessing the power of a relationship based on trust and mutual respect. And it is also based on the realization that the relationship is mutually beneficial. Networking is no different. But you have to know the right people and be friends with them to have a relationship whose power you can harness. And when it comes to transitioning out of the military, that's what it's all about. Domènec Mele concluded in *The Practice of Networking: An Ethical Approach*, "There is nothing wrong in networking to obtain business advantage if one acts with reciprocity when networks are created for mutual benefit or include this option within their ends."[11]

You have to go to great lengths to wash away a bias attached to military service by some people. While a majority of the population respects military service, there are many who believe you will try to bring your military mind-set with you. Lieutenant Commander Bart Denny, US Navy (ret.) found this to be true during his transition to the civilian world. "I found that half of the people I spoke with thought military service was a wonderful asset, and the other half were full of the 'well how do I know you won't be frustrated that you just can't bark out orders that people jump up and follow.'"

This is where networking plays a pivotal role. By getting to know people on a personal level, you can remove any bias they have attached to military service and change their perception. As Lieutenant Commander Denny discovered, "I got a job because I knew people. Plain and simple."

Lieutenant Colonel Riley Hensley, US Army (ret.), considers networking to be personal and akin to friendship. "They call it networking, but I call it just keeping in contact with old friends and associates along life's path. And yes, it did help me land a job later." Never underestimate the value of networking. Think of networking as a business line, only your profits aren't measured in dollars. They're measured by the number of mutually beneficial relationships you form.

Navy veteran Kenisha Thompson concurs with the value and importance of networking:

Networking was a big part of my job search. How many people got out of the navy at the same time I did with the same bag of skills? I had to compete with all of them. Everyone expects military service (especially at the CPO level) to bring with it a certain level of responsibility, diligence, and professionalism; therefore, I needed to sell myself as a person that would fit well with a team. I found that companies wanted to see the person behind the resume.

A great point Kenisha makes is that a lot of people leave the military within similar time frames, so there can be a lot of competition with people who possess similar skill sets and abilities for relatively few jobs. This is true of corporate America as well. Seeing the person behind the resume means getting to know someone and interacting with them—ergo, networking!

Summary

As you begin your transition to the civilian world and your networking journey, set your goals. Write them down. Take stock of who you are and what you can do in a civilian job market. Evaluate what you did, its impact, and the result. Knowing your goals and what you have to offer in the civilian world is the starting point of a networking plan.

Think-It-Through Questions

1. Are my goals consistent with my abilities?
2. Who am I, according to my military experience?
3. What are my circles of influence?
4. Who are the members of my network right now?

CHAPTER TWO

FORM A
COMPREHENSIVE PLAN

~Honest Assessment~

N ow that you have set some goals, taken stock, and assessed your knowledge, skills, and abilities, forming a plan begins with figuring out where you are right now, where you want to go, and how to get there. Then it's a matter of connecting the dots, which may take time, depending on your goals, what you need to do, and what the job market is like.

Jeff Hillegeass was a successful film editor and producer who worked for a nationally syndicated organization. However, when the organization decided to restructure, he was informed that his position had been eliminated. In retrospect, Jeff noted, "I had a plan for the next stage in my back pocket. I determined that a corporate structure and management was not fulfilling to me. I wanted to return to hands on creative work, where I'd achieve a sense of "flow" and time would go by without me being aware of it. To that end, I decided to return to my roots as a Producer and Editor. it was also my intention to be self-employed, so I wouldn't be be held to a single revenue source. I knew I had to re-establish my old contacts, buy equipment (computer, software, peripherals,) name the business, incorporate, teach myself the current technology, etc. I gave myself a generous 15-month window for success. Now, just past 7 months, I'm busier than I ever expected, with a diverse client list." Preparation is the key. As Riley Hensley recalls during his transition from the army, "Assess your situation and the job market first. You have to be realistic on your expectations. Don't rule out an interim (temporary) job either ... the contacts you make may prove priceless later. Always have a resume on hand! And always keep a positive attitude." Hensley correctly notes that attitude is critical. Author John Keller states in his best seller *Attitude Is Everything*, "Your success in life begins and ends with your attitude."[12] Form a *realistic* plan and be positive about it!

An honest assessment of your skills and abilities and what you have to offer a civilian company is critical to knowing what to realistically expect in terms of position and salary. "Be realistic with your expectations for compensation. Know up front what you need to earn to at least maintain your standard of living, and know what you would like to earn to keep your quality of life. Chances are you will land somewhere in the middle, but don't go after a job as a janitor and expect $70,000 a year," says Navy veteran Matt Klym.

Many of us have heard stories about veterans who only spent a few years in the military, got out, and landed a high-paying job. While many of us have heard stories like this, they tend to be little more than urban legends. It's true that in some cases service members have gone on to lucrative positions with what seems like a minimal amount of experience, training, and education, but that is not the norm.

You might want to be a school teacher, but you lack the education and certification. Or you might be considering a career as a crane operator. Perhaps you desire to pursue a career in criminal justice. Regardless of what you want to do, use your source documents to figure out what you *can* do. When you depart the military or your current career, your main objective is to get a job that will pay the bills, so think survival first. Commander A. J. Magnan, US Navy (ret.) offers this advice: "Work hard on the resume, make the resume read like a real job (very little ability for people to translate military skills to everyday skills), start early, be patient and have a supply of cash to live off for a while (3–6 months) while job searching."

~*The Three Plans*~

There are three plans that apply to every service member leaving the military. The first is what I like to call the *dream plan.* As mentioned above, urban legends amount to little more than tall sea stories. Unfortunately, many service members have delusions of grandeur and believe they are going to harness what amounts to little more than above-average experience and training to land a high-paying job or as the catalyst to launch their own business. I have spoken to many service members who thought this way only to have their perspective on reality drastically changed once they were discharged.

The second plan is what I refer to as the *real plan.* This is the plan most service members, including me, do not want to execute. The military trains its personnel for specific jobs. I was trained as a fire controlman. I worked on electronics. It was not my forte, to say the least, but a quick review of my service record and training jacket support my eligibility for a career in the electronics field. Needless to say, that was not what I wanted to do. However, it's what I was trained to do and is something I could earn a paycheck doing. You have to be prepared to take a job you *can* do to pay the bills and support yourself and family (if you have one) while you work on achieving your long-term goals.

The third plan is the most critical—the *survival plan.* This is the plan you will use when you realize the dream plan is just that, a dream, and you've avoided the real plan. Now you're stuck scrambling to collect unemployment compensation and trying to establish a realistic budget.

Here's a quick word on budgets. I was a command financial specialist for seven years. During that time I prepared many budgets for sailors. A budget is not a solution; it's a tool used to identify expenses and determine their legitimacy. Many service members sat in front of me not knowing where their money was going. They actually had little debt and should have had more paycheck left at the end of the month. The problem is they didn't track their expenses or budget for dining out, entertainment, miscellaneous expenses, and so on. Additionally, they didn't realize that a $400 cable bill or a $300 cell phone bill was a bit high, to say the least. Keep those things in mind when you design your survival plan because survival doesn't equal luxury. It means a roof over your head, food on the table, and the bills (the essentials) paid on time.

The three plans above play a vital role in your future. The military trains and prepares you for specific jobs, some of which transfer into the civilian world and some that do not. If what you want to do in the civilian world is reminiscent of your military job, then you should be able to make a fairly easy transition. Doing this successfully, though, requires more than possessing commensurate skills and experience. It too requires networking to get your foot in the door. However, if you want a fresh start in a new career field, your military experience may be minimally helpful, which means you'll be starting from scratch.

~Education vs. Experience~

Look at your chosen field and decide if you need more education, more experience, or both! Then figure out how long it is going to take to get it. The upside of education is that if often yields better job security and a higher salary. The downside is that it takes time, and there are no shortcuts. Education is a great thing—if you know what you want to do with it. But just having a college degree doesn't guarantee employment success, with a company or with your own business. Education is a business that has contributed to the overcredentialing of Americans. A 2011 *New York Times* article titled *The Masters as the New Bachelors* concluded, "the master's is now the fastest-growing degree."[13] As a result, many employers want candidates to have one. Keep that in mind when planning your education. It may take more time to complete the necessary education to meet your goals.

Experience is like education in that it takes time and cannot be acquired any faster than life will allow. Experience, also like education, is not equal. Navy veteran Matt Klym notes, "Experience doesn't always trump education and vice versa." In some career fields, military experience is desired, so that's a plus. However, it may not be required for your chosen field and will perhaps carry little weight. What you may require is more education or certification. Some certifications go a long way, such as Project Management Professional (PMP), Certified Manager, Lean Six Sigma (yellow, green and black belt), Microsoft, Adobe Professional, or other specialized software certification. These take a fraction of the time and expense that education does and can quickly be added to your resume to boost your appeal.

Now, with that said, it's not all about education and certifications, so don't get too caught up in that if you find yourself lacking in those areas. Research professional and fraternal associations, clubs, and organizations affiliated with your particular career field. All fields of business have organizations where collective minds gather, so be sure to get involved. The chamber of commerce is a great place to start and so are Rotary Clubs. While a college degree may go a long way and some certifications are desirable, rubbing elbows with the hiring authority at a local company goes even further.

I worked with a gentleman who recounted a story about how knowing the hiring authority—the *right person*—landed him a great job. He admits that his resume wasn't completely on par with the job listing, but he had worked with the human resources (HR) manager previously. They met over lunch for what he thought would be a brief interview. As it turned out, it lasted several hours, after which he was hired. The irony of the story is that during the interview process, he received an e-mail on his mobile phone from the company's HR department thanking him for applying and informing him that he did not meet the job requirements as listed! The HR manager returned to work and rectified that. Knowing the right people plays a pivotal role in landing a good job, though education and certifications have their place too. Pursuit of those should be part of your long-term plan.

Many of the people I met and spoke with expressed the desire to obtain more education to enhance their chances of finding a good job. Before you jump right into education, take a moment and develop a plan for your education. If you will be starting a bachelor's degree, utilizing your military experience to streamline the process, or are going to pursue a graduate degree, you need to make some critical decisions regarding your education.

The first thing to consider is how you will fund your education. The Montgomery GI Bill is available to veterans as is the Post-9/11 GI Bill. The Post-9/11 GI Bill pays a living allowance and books stipend in addition to covering the cost of tuition. Additionally, many schools participate in the Yellow Ribbon Program. This program provides the means of offsetting the cost should a veteran attend a private institution whose tuition exceeds the covered amount. Something else to consider is that some states offer free or hugely discounted college educations. Verify your state of record *before* you are discharged. You may not be able to change where you entered the military, but you can usually select a new state of record in preparation for discharge. Florida, Texas, and Illinois all offer free college tuition to veterans who are honorably discharged and were residents of the state at the time they entered the military.

For those who do not have access to the GI Bill, there are many scholarships and grants available as well as student loans. A quick search on the Internet will yield a myriad of results and options. Also, many universities, including some top universities, offer hugely discounted tuition. For example, "Though

Harvard's published tuition and fees for the 2011–2012 school year alone totaled $39,849, the 60 percent of students who received need-based aid paid, on average, just $14,495 for tuition and fees, room and board, and other expenses."[14]

Once you decide where you would like to reside after you leave the military, it's time to consider what degree to get. Just like the military, myths and rumors abound about college degrees. Years ago, business was the hot major and would almost guarantee a hefty salary. Today, there is a lot of talk about the information technology (IT) field and its potential to yield a decent income. Before you settle on a major, decide what college you are going to attend. The best advice is to attend the one that meets your needs in terms of cost, major, location, and academic excellence.

We've already discussed the GI Bill, and location will be determined by where you choose to live after your time in the military. That leaves your degree major and the academic excellence to consider. When choosing a major, consider your military training, experience, and whether the education you are pursuing will complement it. For example, if you spent ten years in the medical field, a degree in nursing would certainly complement that. But if you spent six years in the infantry, a degree in education would be difficult to relate. Please understand that your education and experience don't need to complement each other. However, if they do, or if you are leaning toward an education that is somewhat related to your experience, you will have more to offer a potential employer when the time comes.

If you are undecided about a major, consider this. What you choose to major in could be something you love, such as archeology. However, you might be hard pressed to find a decent job with that degree. Conversely, if you choose a major in a demanding and lucrative field, you might make a lot of money but not be happy. So do your research and choose wisely, especially if you are using federal funding. Once it's exhausted, you'll be left with a degree you might not be able to use.

~*The Right People, the Right Associations*~

If you are undecided, a great way to research potential career fields is to utilize professional associations. Doing a quick web search for local chapters of clubs and organizations will provide you with a reference list of places to explore such as the following:

- American Culinary Federation
- American Management Association
- Society for Human Resource Management
- Association of Information Technology Professionals
- International Society of Certified Electronics Technicians
- Association of American Educators

- National Society for Professional Engineers
- American Society for Training and Development
- International Society for Performance Improvement
- National Association of Police Organizations
- American Association of Navy Hospital Corpsman
- National Sonar Association
- U.S. Naval Cryptologic Veterans Association
- Navy League of the United States
- Marine Corps Aviation Association

When you find a few that sound interesting, attend one of their meetings and ask questions of those already in the field. They will be able to tell you about things such as salary, advancement, and what credentials are required in the industry, as well as provide valuable information about the field.

This brings us to the topic of academic excellence. Not everyone can attend a top college, and despite what people may think, the university doesn't necessarily make the man or woman. So don't get hung up on the brand name of a particular university. It's great to have an education, but it's what you do with it that counts. Choose a university you like that meets your needs of location and cost. If you have several that meet those criteria, choose the one that has the best reputation for your chosen field. Again, associations are a great place to glean some of this information.

Additionally, a collective gathering of people interested in a particular field, such as the American Society for Training and Development (ASTD) or a local writer's club, will allow you to compare your experience and knowledge against a civilian standard and determine how you rank against your contemporaries. You may be surprised at what you know and what you can bring to a civilian organization. Membership fees for many associations are nominal (especially for students), but they can reap huge dividends. Remember, your goal is to travel in the right circles and meet the right people.

The right people are the ones who can help you get a job or start your own business, and the right circles are where you can find them. They aren't as elusive or as difficult to get into as you might think. Once you attend a few meetings with different associations, you'll begin to figure out which associations are for you and which ones are not. Many associations allow you to attend as a guest and offer free membership trials. View them as a buffet: sample everything once, but only have seconds of what fits and has potential. This is where you will find the connections you need.

At the invitation of a friend, I attended a seminar sponsored by the American Society for Training and Development. I had a background in training, and my friend thought it would be a great opportunity to broaden my skills and add to my network. It was. I met Paul Ariola, who works for Dale Carnegie Training. Paul and I ran into each other at different events and kept in touch via e-mail. Paul is a navy veteran and understands the difficulties involved in transitioning to the civilian world. I never imagined it at the time we met, but two years later he was my wife's instructor when she took the Dale Carnegie course. Networking makes the world a much smaller place!

After you have assessed your skills and abilities and joined the right associations, it is time to execute your plan. It need not be elaborate, so remember KISS—keep it simple, stupid! Don't try to build a network of a hundred people in a day. It won't work. Rome wasn't built in a day; your network won't be either, so start small. One or two *key* people are all you need to get things rolling. And if you lay your foundation with the right people, they will be more than sufficient for the first step of network construction.

You may have heard that it's the journey that shapes us. When it comes to networking, it's all about the journey and who you meet along the way. You have to know where you want to end up to know with whom to network and where to network, so begin with the end in mind. Remember, the journey of a thousand miles begins with a single step. Just be sure to make the first one count! The first step or, in this case, first addition to your network counts because building a network takes time. It's doubtful that first person is going to be your ticket to a new job. However, that first person might be able to point you in the right direction.

How you start your networking journey will greatly affect its potential. While networking may be an experience, it's one that is undertaken with a specific end in mind. In this case, it's a good job and the potential for upward mobility. And it should also include the goal of continuous growth and expansion to benefit others. A good network continues to grow and lasts a lifetime. It will provide more in terms of employment than anything else at your disposal. The more you add to your network, the greater the yield will be in your future.

Summary

Formulate your plan. It will be a dream plan, a real plan, or a survival plan. Take an accurate assessment of your finances and develop a realistic budget. Decide whether your plan requires education, certification, or both. Search for professional associations to join so you can begin networking with the right people.

Think-It-Through Questions

1. Have I honestly and accurately assessed my knowledge, skills, and abilities?
2. Do I have a survival plan, and is it practical?
3. Do I need education, experience, or both?
4. What associations should I consider joining?

CHAPTER THREE

START PALM
PRESSING EARLY

~The People You Know~

With networking, it's not about the people you know. It's about the people *they* know! The people with whom you network may not be able to do anything *directly* to help you get a job or advance your career. However, they may know someone who can, and that's the key to networking—choosing the right people. In his 2002 book, *The Tipping Point*, Author Malcolm Gladwell calls these people "connectors." "The first—and most obvious—criterion is that connectors know lots of people. They are the kinds of people who know everyone. Connectors are important for more than simply the number of people they know.

Their importance is also a function of the kinds of people they know."[15] In my case, Dave Boisselle was my connector. He put me in contact with literally dozens of people, many of whom proved to be vital contacts in not only helping myself, but also in helping others.

Building a network takes time but can grow exponentially after meeting just a few people. Don't concern yourself with trying to meet one or two key people at the top of an organization. In the words of Ivan Misner, founder of BNI, "One metaphor I like is that most people treat networking like hunting—they're out there trying to bag the big one—but it's really a lot more like farming. You have to cultivate relationships over time."[16] So get out there and start planting seeds.

At the same time, don't neglect your existing networks. The networks you currently have can prove invaluable as you begin a new chapter of your life. Jeff Hillegass notes,

In a nutshell, I've found that if you want to tap into something in your past, and your current network can't see you in that light, you have to work with your old network and with a new network you create in the progress. Every place I work (or every client who sends me material) is a chance to reconnect with those from the past, and get acquainted with new people on the projects. Eventually, my old network and the new larger network created from reconnecting will crossover with my most recent network, and the process of recreating myself will be complete.

Scout local universities, union halls, and job fairs. Remember, they may not be able to help you find a job at their institutions, but they may very likely know someone who can. Once you meet some of the right people, find out what the current trends are in your field—what's hot and what's not. Research trade journals and associations. Make contact with local organizations and companies. Consider volunteer work. Volunteer work doesn't cost you anything but time, and you never know whom you might meet. You can volunteer for charities, churches, public radio stations, your local YMCA or SPCA, or a host of other organizations. You want your name to be out there, and the best way to do it is by making contact with the right people at key organizations. Who is leading your industry? What company offers benefits that suit your needs? Who are the subject-matter experts? They say familiarity breeds contempt, but with networking it breeds recognition and exposure.

It is never too early in your career to start attending professional luncheons. I started attending Regent University's Executive Leadership Series (ELS) luncheons shortly after I realized I might be transitioning. The first time I went, my reason was simple: I wanted to hear John Maxwell speak. I had read several of his books, and because

I was on limited duty, I had the time. What I realized at my first luncheon was the power of mingling with business leaders. These were people who had the connections for me to get a job. Breaking into this sphere of influence wasn't going to be easy, but it wasn't as difficult as you might think. One of the first people I met after the luncheon was Dr. Carlos Campo, the newly inaugurated president of Regent University. I made it a point to introduce myself to him and to tell him a little bit about myself (I am a Regent alumnus) and my goal of speaking there after I completed my doctorate degree (some four years away at the time). I also met former Chief of Naval Operations Admiral Vern Clark at the ELS.

I saw Dr. Campo at subsequent luncheons each month and at various university functions. I took just enough time to say hello, nothing more. After several luncheons and brief conversations, he began to know my face. Recognition! This is a critical step because recognition leads to conversation, and conversation leads to discovering common ground. At the Regent luncheon, John Maxwell spoke about effective communication and said, "Effective communication is about finding common ground and connecting."[17] Be recognizable and you are well on your way to taking the next step of finding common ground.

You can easily find common ground by ascertaining critical information about your chosen field from the companies and people in the field and using it to get out there to meet the *right* people! These are the companies and people you want to have your resume. They are the ones you want to meet every month at the Rotary Club, training seminars, professional luncheons, or even the local gym. Recognition is the impetus to conversation. Be seen and recognized frequently by the key people in your field.

As Michael Douglas's character, Gordon Gekko, said in the 1987 movie *Wall Street*, "The most valuable commodity I know of is information." Even though he was not speaking about networking, truer words were never spoken. If you go into an interview with hardly a clue about what the company does, don't expect to knock anyone's socks off when asked about the company. But if you do your research, perhaps make a few phone calls, and conduct some research about the company that isn't widely known, you are sure to make a favorable impression when asked about the company.

Now apply that same philosophy to networking. When you research companies, pay attention to key people, such as the HR manager. Read the biography, if available, search the company website, and make a few phone calls to the HR office. Talk to the hiring manager, if you can, although some companies keep this a closely guarded secret, and the department manager. Neil McNulty, founder of McNulty Management and a marine corps veteran, recommends contacting the HR manager, president, or chief executive officer directly. Sometimes going straight to the top gets you noticed and makes an impression. With that said, don't forget about receptionists, assistants, and other gatekeepers. They can be even more important than the big fish.

Learn what you can about the person who might be interviewing you. Research people when you meet them so that if and when you meet again, you can ask a specific question or two out of the ordinary. This is where connectors come into play. If you know a connector, chances are that he or she can provide you with information that is more specific and personal about someone in a hiring position. This makes mingling and small talk easier and more rewarding.

Another great place to mix and mingle with your own kind and to make contacts is job fairs. They are offered in many locations throughout the country, so you should be able to find one in your area. Websites such as www.corporategray.com provide e-mail notices about local job fairs if you subscribe to their mailing list. Subscribe! You may not walk away with a job, but at the very least you will make contact with the right people and get your name *out there*! Additionally, by talking with many of the corporate recruiters, you can become comfortable talking with people from this new world you're about to enter.

~*Papers Please*~

Before you attend a job fair, get your playbook ready. The disadvantage of job fairs is that you don't have the option of writing a detailed resume. You're stuck writing a general resume, which may or may not hit the mark with anyone. Although this is a disadvantage, it is overshadowed by the opportunity to meet a large number of people from many companies. However, you still need to refine your resume so that it's not too general and not too specific. You want to give any potential employer an accurate picture of who you are, where you've been, and what you have to offer for a variety of positions. It takes time and practice. Have friends and colleagues review it for you and provide honest feedback. Fleet and Family Service Centers provide resume writing classes and will critique your resume. Take advantage of these services.

In addition to your resume, you will need a business card such as the one in the example below. You can have them printed by a litany of companies available locally or on the web. What you need to do is ensure that it contains the *right* information. The right information gives a potential employer a snapshot of who you are and what you have to offer. Think of it as a condensed resume. It's your ten-second commercial telling someone why he or she should hire you and not the other person. To that end, it should reflect your best qualities and qualifications.

For example, if you have a college degree, list that because many jobs require a certain level of education. Do you have a special qualification or certification? List that too. Also, list your military service. Why? A lot of jobs in the military require a clearance, which conveys a certain amount of trust. Employers want trustworthy people, and they want reliable people who will show up on time and do what is required. A successful tour in the military indicates you are capable of those things.

Your business card should allow a potential employer to check off several items on a job listing. You should list competencies that align with the industry you are seeking (Figure3.1). It is of critical importance, so equate it with American Express: "Don't leave home without it!" Don't run to the supermarket or McDonald's without a business card. Keep a few cards in your pocket at all times. Networking is a full-time job and can happen *anywhere*! Be prepared. In military jargon, think of it as part of your uniform. Speaking of which, it's important to look professional all the time. Rather than run out in jeans and a T-shirt, opt for khakis and a polo shirt. You never know who you'll run into, so look the part all the time.

John T. Smith, PMP U.S. Navy (ret.)
Certified Project Manager
City, State johntsmith@gmail.com (123) 456-7890

Figure 3.1. A sample business card.

Believe it or not, there is such a thing as business card etiquette. What this means is that you do not walk into a room, start shaking hands with everyone, and immediately ask them for their business cards. The object is not to see how many you can collect. Quality is what matters most, not quantity. As my colleague Philip Foster notes, "A business card is meant to be an extension of the conversation." In other words, you need to take the time to get to know some- one before offering your card (and hopefully receiving one in return). You may find that you do not want or need it after engaging in conversation with an individual. Conversely, the same applies. Don't walk into a room and start handing your business card out like a blackjack dealer in Las Vegas. Most of them will surely find their way to the trash can.

One of the key pieces of information on your business card is your e-mail address. We live in a digital age, and the majority of our communication is now done via e-mail. Therefore, your e-mail address should be professional, not humorous or suggestive. It conveys a message, so choose wisely. I recommend using Gmail for job searches and professional correspondence; use Hotmail or Yahoo for friends and family. Additionally, even though you may have given someone your business card, you will want to create a signature block on your e-mail that mirrors your business card. You might be inclined to send an e-mail to someone you met at a luncheon, and you want to ensure he has all of your information at the ready when your e-mail is read rather than his having to fumble around for it. Business cards make regular trips through laundry machines, are often discarded with other papers by accident, or get filed away in an organizer never to be seen again. So reinforce your contact information with a signature block (Figure 3.2).

Sincerely,

John T. Smith, PMP
U.S. Navy (ret.)
Certified Professional Manager
Virginia Beach, VA
(123) 456-7890

Figure 3.2. A sample e-mail signature block.

~*Run for Office*~

We've all seen politicians on the campaign trail shaking hands with the voters. They smile enthusiastically as they work the crowd. Voters watch with admiration of their energy and positivity. With networking, *you* are now the politician, so you need to learn how to work the crowd and greet people with enthusiasm.

There are two critical components when greeting people you don't know: looking the part and acting like you belong there. Although a large portion of military personnel are extroverts, not everyone is an extrovert all the time or on all occasions. Approaching new people is often difficult, especially for those who are passive, but it's not impossible. First, you have to look the part. That is, you must present a professional appearance—well groomed, suit, tie, shoes shined, and so on. As noted by Great Britain's Queen Victoria in a letter to Edward, Prince of Wales (1851), and is still true today: "Dress gives on the outward sign from which people in general can, and often do, judge the inward state of mind and feelings of a person; for this they can see while the other they cannot see.[18]

Second, you have to act like you belong there. In other words, you shouldn't feel uneasy. Instead, you must *act* as though everyone in the room is there to meet *you*. I know that sounds like a stretch, but it's how you have to think or you'll miss golden opportunities. The former president of Regent University's Student Veterans Association recounted a story to me about an internship she did. At one point in the internship, she attended a breakfast sponsored by the Republican National Convention. When she was introduced to people with whom she could have connected and networked, she

demurred because she felt the other people were more important than her. A golden opportunity was lost, but a valuable
lesson was learned. Look and act the part at all times because
you are running for office, and you need votes!

Third, when you enter an event, canvas the room and
survey the field. Which people seem to have a crowd
gathered around them? Who is getting the most attention?
These are the people you want to get to know. Find a way to
introduce yourself and to speak to them. Remember, these
are the people who are well connected and are the ones you
are there to meet and greet, as it were.

~To-Do List~

You may be one of those people who chats with people
at the grocery store and can strike up a conversation with
anyone. That is a plus and will definitely help you. However,
when you engage in conversation with the intent of networking, there are some key things you want to do—and not do!

Things to do:
1. *Smile.* A friendly smile is always welcome and is
   contagious.
2. *Look people in the eye.* Have you ever tried to hold a
   conversation with someone who doesn't look at you
   when you speak? Besides being annoying, it's not
   conducive to good networking. If you're one of those

people, practice looking people in the eye when you speak to them.

3. *Focus on them.* In a large group setting, it's easy to get distracted when engaging in conversation. Perhaps you see someone out of the corner of your eye with whom you want to speak or maybe you're looking for someone. When you speak with others, your focus on them should be so intense that they feel like the most important person in the room.

4. *Censure yourself.* Many lengthy and stimulating conversations begin with small talk, that is, speaking about things such as the local sports teams or current events. While such banter is usually friendly in nature, it can quickly turn offensive if you speak aggressively about topics such as politics or religion and turn into an argument. As Dale Carnegie states, "The only argument you will win is the one you don't have."[19] You might be able to voice your opinion to your friends and family, but when you network, remain neutral and cordial. If asked for an opinion, be honest, but do so with a high degree of discretion and tact. For example, if asked about a particular government official's performance, you might state, "I believe he is doing the best job possible under the circumstances" versus "I think he is doing a terrible job and should be removed from office." It may not be natural to do this, but it's something you must to

71

learn to do to be an effective leader and networker. After all, you can't add people to your network if you are busy offending them.

Things not to do:

1. *Don't interrupt.* When you speak with people, *listen* to them. Many times during conversations we tend to think about what we want to say, which is why we often miss important pieces of information. This preoccupation with our own thoughts is what leads to interruptions. Once you form the habit of interrupting someone, it's hard to break. Constantly interrupting essentially tells someone you really aren't paying attention or focusing on what is being said. If you continually interrupt someone, you'll never get to know him or her and be able to network effectively.

2. *Don't check your phone.* Cell phones and personal data devices are ubiquitous in today's business environment. At a minimum, cell phone ringers should be off at an interview or networking event. Set it to vibrate if you must be reachable. However, if you can go without it, do so. One of the biggest distracters is the constant checking of e-mails and text messages. When you reach for your phone during a conversation, you're conveying to the person with whom you're speaking that what they are saying really isn't important or worthy of your full attention. If you

should receive a phone call during a conversation, ignore it. Unless it could be a possible emergency call, let whoever is calling leave a message and call them back. This enables you to give your full attention to the person in front of you and to the person who is calling when you return the call. Allowing phone calls and texts to distract you while engaging in conversation is inconsiderate and rude, and it's contrary to good networking practices. Also, avoid silly ringtones. If you must have your phone ringer on, always keep things professional.

3. *Don't use inappropriate language.* Members of the military have a reputation for using foul language as part of their everyday lexicon. While this may be true to a certain extent, such language has no place in a networking environment. Networking is a professional business and requires professional dialogue. Even if the person to whom you are speaking uses profane language, don't follow suit and feel that you can join in. Professionalism is always in vogue.

4. *Don't check your watch.* What message is conveyed by someone looking at his or her watch while you are talking to him or her? Perhaps you are checking the time so you aren't late for a meeting, but tell that to the person who is speaking to you. Checking your watch sends the message that you want you to end your conversation because it is taking up too much

of your valuable time. Your time is valuable, and so is theirs. Spending your time to focus and talk with others shows them how valuable they are.

5. *Don't discuss inappropriate topics.* When meeting people for the first time, the last thing you want to do is give a negative impression. Avoid topics such as sex and other divisive subjects. You will quickly alienate yourself from the crowd by voicing your opinion about such topics. We live in a politically correct age. Therefore, adhere to good standards and practice proper decorum at all times, even if those in your group do not. Their participation is not an invitation for you to do the same.

You might be thinking that's a lot of information to remember and put into practice. It is. Instead of trying to practice everything at your next networking event, focus on the basics. Walk up to people, smile, and introduce yourself: "Hi, I'm [pause] Bill. How are you?" Pausing for just a brief second focuses the attention of the other person on what you are saying by creating an expectation. It tells the other person you are about to say something important.

As you gain experience networking, focus on the other dos and don'ts. Although they may sound like common sense, they actually take some time to hone and polish. We all like to talk about ourselves. If you're not careful, you'll soon be telling your life story to someone just because they asked you a simple question or two. Focusing on the other person is deliberate, purposeful, and must be practiced. Ridding yourself of bad habits takes time and effort but can be accomplished in a short amount of time if you work at it. The benefit is that you will be better communicator.

After you have had the opportunity to get out there and mingle, honestly evaluate how you did. A simple way of doing this is by remembering everything you can from a few conversations. How much do you know about the people who gave you their business cards? Do you think they know more about you than you do about them? Who did most of the talking? Did you find yourself eagerly waiting for them to stop talking so you could say something? Did you remember their name when you saw them later, and if so, did you call them by name? Asking yourself these basic types of questions can quickly reveal the effectiveness of your networking ability. Don't be surprised if you don't do well the first few times. It takes practice, and you will learn from experience.

Summary

Networking is about getting to know people and forming relationships. Do your research about potential employers, prepare your resume, and always have a business card in your pocket. Adhere to the dos and don'ts and you'll be ready to start building your network.

Think-It-Through Questions

1. Who are all the people I know, and how do I know them?
2. What do my resume and business card say about me?
3. Do I look and act the part?
4. Do I know what to do and what not to do to effectively network?

CHAPTER FOUR

BUILDING THE SPIDER WEB

~Connect with People~

I f you talk to anyone who is looking for a job, they will invariably tell you they are busy sending resumes out in response to job listings. Well, that's one way to get a job, and it does work in a number of situations. However, the people I spoke with who recently went through the transition from the military to the civilian world overwhelmingly claimed this was a labor-intensive process that often yielded little results. Many stated they would get called in for an interview only to be disappointed weeks later with a subpar offer that was not comparable to their skills and ability. Again, as discussed in chapter one, it's important that your skills and ability are accurately reflected on your resume.

As you travel on your networking journey to find a new job or start a business, you will meet many people. These people are what Gladwell refers to as "acquaintances." He notes, "The purpose of making acquaintances, for most of us, is to evaluate whether we want to turn that person into a friend; we don't feel we have the time or the energy to maintain meaningful contact with everyone."[20] This is true; however, when it comes to networking, you need to tap into your reserve energy and make time for others because you never know where a relationship will lead. One way to streamline this process is to keep track of the acquaintances you meet.

The business card exchange occurs on cue regularly at job fairs, luncheons, seminars, and the occasional unexpected meeting. Soon you will have quite a pile of cards sitting on your desk, and you'll be wondering what to do with all of them. Some people file them in a business card organizer. These are great for organizing your take-out dining choices or keeping track of infrequently used phone numbers such as the plumber, but they're not well suited for networking.

When I started networking, I quickly realized the value of keeping track of those with whom I came into contact. I began taping business cards on the top of a page in a Moleskine notebook. I wrote all the information I could remember about the person under the card, including where we met, the date, and personal information, if known, such as where they were from, favorite authors, where they went to school, and so forth. I also annotated any correspondence I sent them, the type—e-mail, letter, or card—and the date. This quickly became part of my standard operating procedure, and I still use it today.

This technique allowed me to review how often I communicated with my network on a regular basis. As mentioned previously, communication is essential. Frequency is vital too. Too much communication makes you a pest. Too little makes you a stranger. Again, it's all about finding the right balance. It takes time, but you will get a feel for it as you go, based on the person and the relationship. You won't communicate with everyone with the same frequency, so don't start a regimen of sending e-mails every week for the sake of sending them just to stay in contact. You should also not set up reminders on your electronic calendar to e-mail someone unless, of course, it is for a specific purpose such as a birthday or anniversary. Communicate as necessary for a valid reason, and use your networking book as a guide. I'll discuss this in a later chapter.

As you start tracking your network, you will begin to learn a great deal about others. Bingo! That's what networking is all about—people. Networking, if done correctly, makes you a better communicator because learning about other people requires you to ask questions and be a good listener. Dale Carnegie knew all too well that people love to talk about themselves and what interests them. Keep that in mind when you meet new people. John Maxwell told the story of one of the best communicators he'd ever met. At a dinner party, she steered the conversation back to the person with whom she was speaking when she was asked questions. This caused the other person to talk about himself or herself and provided a plethora of information to add to her networking book. She was regarded as an incredibly hospitable host.[21]

Communicating with people is about connecting with them and finding common ground. To do that, you need information. Where did they grow up? What's their favorite hobby? What authors do they like? Getting to know someone allows you to connect with him or her. Once you connect, you can begin to network. So keep track of all their information and remember such details as anniversaries and birthdays. Make note of them in your networking book.

~*The Personal Touch*~

Dale Carnegie advocated sending someone a birthday card every year.[22] Well, when it comes to networking, it's *always* someone's birthday, so send a card! And don't limit yourself to just birthdays. Holidays are a great time to send a card. Don't forget to put a business card inside. Write a personal note on the back. Connect with them. Networking is like luck. It's all in the cards! Keep track of holidays and birthdays, and remember to consult your networking book for details. A card that says, "Have a great Christmas. I know Santa will be good to your son and daughter," will go a long way. And a birthday card that indicates you know it's the recipient's thirtieth birthday shows you pay attention and do your homework.

A card brightens a person's day and lets him or her know you care in a way an e-mail cannot. And it might just be the one thing that separates you from everyone else and gets a response. A friend of mine had been going through a rough time a while back. I sent several e-mails offering encouragement but received no response, so I sent a card. Here is the response I received:

> I got your card—thank you for being persistent. I've been really bad at writing people lately, and the card made me feel better. I got it last week when I was home sick with a fever of about 103, chills ...so suffice it to say, it made my day.

Taking the time to send a hand-written card can brighten someone's day and lift his or her spirits. It can also be the one thing that separates you from your contemporaries and gets you noticed. I had the opportunity to sit with Jan Helvie, events producer and administrator for Regent University, at a luncheon. We talked at length afterward, and when everyone had gone, she began to clear off some of the flower centerpieces on the tables. Knowing from our discussion that I have twin girls and a wife at home, she gave me some flowers to take with me. When I got home, I immediately sent a thank-you note. Here is her response:

> I also received your very warm hand-written note today! Wow! Such a lost art. Thank you doubly for taking the time to do THAT!!!

It's no wonder seven billion greeting cards are purchased each year. Never underestimate the power of a hand-written note. It tells them they were worth taking the time to fill out a card, address it, put postage on it, and place it in the mail, which, as Jan describes it, is a "lost art"!

Use the cyber touch too. Many people are on Facebook today, so add them as your friends. However, be mindful of the information you post and share. Consider it the IT department of your network. You might learn a little more about them that allows you to connect with them. Unlike Facebook, LinkedIn is strictly a networking tool. You can use it to post your resume and career history as well as to search for people in your particular industry and region. It features a message service that provides your connections with an e-mail whenever your profile changes. Log on and get connected. Connecting and networking go hand-in-hand. Remember that.

A word of caution about using social networks is appropriate. You have probably heard the saying that "Perception is nine-tenths reality." Essentially it means that what people see, they think and make reality. While many of us like to post pictures and links on Facebook, what we post is who we are. So, if you are using a social network, use a liberal amount of discretion and consider those who might view what you post. A potential job offer could quickly be lost due to a shared opinion that is considered offensive. Many HR managers and job recruiters review the social networks of applicants, so use discretion.

I am guilty of this and speak from experience. It's easy to get carried away and post what you intend to be timely and informative information. However, once you post it, it becomes who you are and what you stand for and is now someone else's perception about your reality. Before you know it, that wonderful contact you made at a luncheon has blocked you. Therefore, don't use social networking sites as your personal soapbox to make controversial comments. If you are going to invite people you meet to be your friend or follow you, use common sense and carefully scrutinize what you post. If you have any doubt, *don't* post it!

~*A Degree or Two*~

As you begin to construct your network (spider web), you will be surprised at how many new people you meet. In fact, you might become overwhelmed. Relax. It's okay. For the most part, you can never know too many people. There's a saying about publicity. All publicity is good publicity. Some celebrities are living proof of that because they manage to stay in the limelight, and usually not for good reasons. But people are quick to read about them and their exploits, aren't they?

Well, networking is the same way. Meeting new people is good for your network regardless of who they are, so don't fret when you mingle and find yourself knowing a dozen people you never knew before. The key is to remember that everyone knows someone, and while that may seem a little obvious and rhetorical, that's what networking is all about—knowing people who know people who know the *right* people.

We've all heard the term "six degrees of separation," which essentially connects two unknown people through six people they know. The notion of six degrees of separation grew out of work conducted by the social psychologist Stanley Milgram in the 1960s. Milgram decided to investigate the so-called small-world problem, the hypothesis that everyone on the planet is connected by just a few intermediaries. In his experiments, a few hundred people from Boston and Omaha tried to get a letter to a target—a complete stranger in Boston. But they could only send the letter to a personal friend whom they thought was somehow closer to the target than they were. When Milgram looked at the letters that reached the target, he found that they had changed hands only about six times. This finding has since been encapsulated in the notion that *everyone* can be connected by a chain of acquaintances roughly six links long.[23]

Well, my friends, that's true of networking as well. The contacts you make at the local job fair or chamber of commerce meeting might not be able to do anything to help you, but they might have a friend who knows the director of personnel at a company that's perfect for you. You get the idea. A recent article in *Entrepreneur Magazine* discussed the importance of this very topic:

> The value that you bring to a referral network or to a strategic alliance is directly related to the number of relationships you have and the quality of those relationships. In a typical referral-networking group of 20 to 40 people, the number of referrals that could be created, among all the possible contacts within one or two degrees of separation, is almost incalculable. And it doesn't take a corporate executive to connect you with another corporate executive, or a rich person to introduce you to

another rich, influential person. That's not the way the world works anymore — and quite honestly, I'm not sure it ever was.[24]

View all the people you meet as that first degree of separation and figure out how to connect the dots. You might just be surprised at how many people you have in common and to whom they might be connected.

For example, I graduated from Regent University with a gentleman who, as it turned out, is friends with someone I later met at an alumni breakfast. I didn't know it at the time, but as my friend Kent and I got to know each other at several meetings and gatherings after the alumni breakfast, I discovered he knows my friend Matthew. I also discovered that Kent is friends with a gentleman at my church, Brent, and Brent knows Baxter, who was the executive director of events and university relations at Regent. I saw him every month at the ELS and other university functions and got to know him. Dots were starting connect as to who knew whom. Later, at another luncheon, I met Rhonda, who also knows Kent and Brent from the same Rotary Club. Rhonda unknowingly gave me a golden nugget about networking that I hadn't realized. She said, "The majority of the people at this luncheon all belong to the same associations." How about that? Birds of a feather *do* flock together. It's time to spread your wings!

~*Worth the Price*~

Now, I know what you're saying. Joining all of these associations and attending these luncheons and seminars costs money. Yes, they sure do. But as with anything that is worthwhile, you have to give to get. There is no free lunch, and that is especially true with networking. As my friend Dave always says, "You've got to have some skin in the game." A successful network is mutually beneficial and balanced, but that takes time. Your network, much like a business, is in the start-up phase. For now, seize networking opportunities with a vengeance! Pony up and pay the price for a luncheon or membership into your local Rotary chapter or chamber of commerce. It's a relatively minor investment that will reap huge dividends.

Learn to talk to everyone with whom you come into contact. Call it schmoozing or whatever you like, but take the time to know people, especially at places you frequent. Do you belong to a gym? Chat up the people who work there. I know most of the people who work at my gym and greet them by name every time I see them. Remember, it's all about them in the conversation, so ask questions, smile, and most importantly remember their names! Call them by name every time you see them and ask them questions about themselves. "How was your weekend?" " Did you go anywhere for Thanksgiving?" "I haven't seen you in a while, were you on vacation?" And most importantly, *remember* what they tell you. That is perhaps the most difficult part of networking. It's a challenge to recall that information at a moment's notice, but you can train your mind to do it. Work on it, because once you master it, you will be the one *they* remember! As Dale Carnegie said, you have to become *genuinely* interested in people.[25]

I belong to a local gym, and I would take my daughters swimming on Saturdays. I got to know the lifeguard. We spoke on occasion and became familiar with each other. Whenever she was there, I always said hi and called her by name. Well, one Saturday while I was swimming with my daughters, who were three at the time, she came over and gave them each a little toy duck to play with. They thought that was great. So did I! As time passed, we spoke more frequently. There were several occasions where she looked out for my interests either by taking the time to provide me with relevant information or to make sure the sauna was hot enough. And it all started with a smile and a name! Networking opportunities are everywhere. Be proactive and seek them out.

Building a network is analogous to creating a new life. Once conceived, it must be fed regularly to become healthy, strong, and mature. "Effective networking is about building relationships with others who can refer you once they've come to trust you, have confidence in you and feel loyal to you. This truly is the key to networking success. And this process takes time,"[26] states Ivan Misner in *The*

Key to Networking. A great way to build and strengthen any relationship is through regular, purposeful contact. In other words, contact people for a reason. That reason could simply be to say hello or to inquire about their life or job. Whatever you do, don't make the mistake of contacting them to tell them about *yourself* and what's going on with your life.

Sure, friends call to chat about their problems, discuss their dreams, and vent. And, yes, you are trying to eventually become friends with many of the people in your network, but this is a *professional* relationship you are building. There are boundaries, so treat your contact with those in your network accordingly. Remember Dale Carnegie's famous words, "People love to talk about themselves,"[27] when you make contact. This applies to you too, so keep it in check. Ask questions and listen to what people tell you.

~*It's Not about You*~

Another great way to strengthen your network and add value to it is to bring something of value to others, which is what servant leadership is all about. President John F. Kennedy understood this concept well. It is demonstrated in his famous words, "Ask not what your country can do for you—ask what you can do for your country."[28] The same holds true with your network and those in it. Start thinking in terms of what you can do for others. Who can you bring into your network? Who in your network needs help? The more you give to those in your network, the more you will receive in return, and the stronger it will become. This is truly the greatest benefit of networking and will make your network self-sustaining.

In the movie *Field of Dreams,* Kevin Costner, as Ray Kinsella, was told, "If you build it, they will come."[29] Well, guess what? The same is true of a network. If you build a strong, viable network, others will join it. Find that hard to believe? Just look at the networks you've joined that someone else built as evidence. Networks attract people because networks are about people with common interests. When you build one, especially one that is mutually beneficial, people will come. And the more people who join your network, the stronger it will become.

As you begin to meet people and add them to your network, remember to make it only as big as it needs to be. Some people have a tendency to think more is better. That mentality is prevalent in our society, but it's not necessarily true for networks. Networks are about quality relationships, and you can't build quality relationships with a large group of people in a short period of time. In fact, according to Malcolm Gladwell's research for *The Tipping Point*, "The figure of 150 seems to represent the maximum number of individuals with whom we can have a genuinely social relationship, the kind of relationship that goes with knowing who they are and how they relate to us."[30] So once your network is self-sustaining, add people only as necessary. In time it will grow and comprise many people, and you will be able to develop strong, meaningful relationships with many, if not all, of the people in it. But you won't be able to do that right away. Networking is a full-time job, so use discretion and control your appetite. Although many people might fit the mold, not everyone needs to be part of your network. Be selective.

Summary

Networking is all in the cards. Keep track of the business cards you receive. Send a card and use the power of a hand-written note. Be professional in your social media activity because someone is always looking. Survey the field carefully because we're only separated by six degrees of separation. Bring value to others and your network will continue to grow as you pursue new endeavors at home.

Think-It-Through Questions

1. How will I effectively communicate with and track those in my network?
2. Are my social networks professional?
3. How many people separate me from the people I need to know?
4. How can I add value to the lives of others?

CHAPTER FIVE

DRY GROUND

~Increasing in Value~

I n navy parlance, you made it ashore—you're going home. You found a job, took your first steps in a new career, or started your own business. Great. Now what? Months, or perhaps even a year ago, you started networking and built your network with the purpose of meeting the right people so you could find the job of your dreams or start your own enterprise. Your hard work paid off. Sure, you could sever ties with the people who helped you get your job or get started on your own or you could simply become passive and allow the network to die on the vine from lack of care. The thought of abandoning your network might cross your mind, especially if you got into networking for the wrong reasons. Your network, though, was once a diamond in the rough that you stumbled upon by accident. You cared for it, shaped it, and polished it, thereby increasing its value to both you and those in it.

A young copywriter working for N. W. Ayer & Son, Frances Gerety, coined the famous advertising line "A diamond is forever" in 1947. In 2000, *Advertising Age* magazine named "A diamond is forever" the best advertising slogan of the twentieth century.[31] Just like a diamond, a network is forever too. So once you create a network, you need to appraise it regularly and insure it because it will only increase in value—like a diamond.

How does a network increase in value? Simple. Your network will increase in value by attracting more people and serving their needs. For any network to have value, it must contain two elements: people and benefit. As I mentioned at the beginning of this book, when you first start networking, you do so with the intent of having the network help you. Along the way, you quickly realize you have something of value to offer others and have the capacity to help them through your network. This is what gives all networks value and sustains them—reciprocity.

This premise of reciprocity is crucial to good networking and has not changed in decades. It's an underpinning of successful interactions and communication, whether face-to-face or online. "The effective, powerful people we know just know a lot of people. They can contact them, interact and make things happen on our behalf in a way that can contribute to our business growth. And we must return the favor,"[32] states Susan RoAne.

Think of reciprocity as compound interest. We've all heard the expression "let your money work for you," meaning let your money make money via compound interest through investment. When you invest in people, you invest in your network. In turn, your network works for you. It compounds in value just like money in a savings account. In just a short amount of time, your initial investment can be worth double its value, and with networking, it can double in value many times over. As your network increases in size and dimension, it will add value to other people's lives.

John Maxwell notes in *The Twenty-One Irrefutable Laws of Leadership,* "We add value to others when we make ourselves more valuable to others. The whole idea of adding value to other people depends on the idea that you have something of value to add."[33] In this case, what you have to offer others is your network and those in it.

I was at a luncheon and was introduced to a freshly retired coast guard officer. After thirty years with the coast guard, he was overwhelmed by the civilian world. His quest to find a job had been fruitless. Even more disturbing was the realization that after so much time in the bubble of the military, he was ill prepared to navigate his way through the job-hunting process. He was applying all the techniques he'd learned at TAP, mailing resumes and cover letters and knocking on doors, with little result.

Even though I had only barely begun my networking journey, I saw an opportunity to add value to his life. I was able
to add value to his life because I had something to offer—my
network—and I was perceived, for perhaps the first time, as
having something of value to add. I spent several hours with him
after the luncheon, reviewing the principles in this book. We
corresponded regularly via e-mail and got together regularly to
catch up and discuss ways for him to strategize as he continued
his job search. He found a terrific job, and I'm still in regular
contact with him today. He frequently e-mails me job opportunities that are conducive to my skills, abilities, and interest.

Adding value to someone's life is an incredible experience because it's more than just helping someone. Helping
someone tends to be for a short duration. I was *leading*
someone, and this is one of the ways networking is all about
leadership. When I first started networking, others led me.
As I became more proficient at it and developed my own
network, I started to lead others. Once you begin to lead
others, your network grows and gains value. It begins to
attract people and starts to work for you and them. This is
the time to appraise it and insure it.

~What It's Worth~

Appraising your network is not unlike appraising a
diamond or other valuable collectable. The only difference is
that *you* do the appraising rather than taking it to an outside

entity. Remember that Moleskine notebook I mentioned? Open your networking book, address book, computer file, or whatever you've been using to track people and review it. Are you in regular contact with everyone? How long has it been since you corresponded with someone? Just because you haven't corresponded with certain people in a while doesn't mean it's time to remove them from your network. This is the perfect time to drop someone a line just to say hi, see how they are doing, and reconnect. Everyone in your network is valuable, but at the same time a network that is too large cannot be effectively managed, which means it will begin to lose benefit and value. As mentioned in chapter four, the ideal number of people one person can effectively associate with is 150.

It's unlikely your network will become that large within a short time, but some people have a knack for it and can expand their networks quickly. Keep your network in check and keep track of its size. When you appraise it, first look at its size. Is it manageable? If the number of people in your network is manageable, there is no need to remove anyone from it.

The tougher issue, if it is unmanageable, is to determine if you really need everyone in it. This is difficult because, as we have seen, networking is a leadership issue, and we often feel that once we begin leading people we should continue to lead them. However, this is not necessarily the case. Some people only require brief direction and involvement and, once shown, are able to continue on their way independently. You may find that to be the case with many people in your network.

You may also find that you don't click with everyone you meet. That may sound rather obvious, but I've found that many people feel discouraged when they don't mesh well with everyone they meet at networking events. We are all different in various ways. The point of networking isn't to get along with everyone you meet. Rather, the point is to simply meet and be cordial with as many people as possible. In a room full of people, you might click with only a handful of people. That's okay. The key is to meet as many people as you can so you can find people with similar interests and thus collaborate. Concentrate on meeting people. You'll know who is a fit and who isn't and will develop an instinct for discerning that.

Another criterion for appraising your network is to evaluate those who are still active in it. Networking is a reciprocal relationship, a two-way street. If you find you are doing all the giving and another is doing all the taking, you really aren't networking. Though many relationships in a network start out this way, they quickly develop into reciprocal relationships. If they don't, it may be time to reassess a member's value and intentions.

You can also appraise your network by examining the nature of the relationships within it. We often think of a network as a large, single, encompassing group. For example, imagine a room with a hundred or so people in it. This represents your network. Contained within this group, though, are subgroups. You've seen this at luncheons, receptions, banquets, and so forth. The room is filled with them. Three people are huddled in a corner talking; five or six stand in the center chatting; a large group is off to the side laughing and smiling; and so the pattern goes throughout the room. Your network is composed of many subnetworks. So while you might lead someone, that is, connect someone, from one subgroup to another, there may no longer be a *continued* need to remain active with that person. The nature of the relationship changed. It has served its purpose and requires no further involvement from you.

There are no hard and fast rules to tell you who to keep and who to let go. That is a matter of individual conscience. However, if you use the guidance above, you will be able to make the difficult decision easier by quantifying and qualifying it, and thus make a fair appraisal.

~Stay in Touch~

Once you've appraised your network, it's time to insure it. Insuring a network isn't like insuring a car or house. Insurance agents don't offer coverage for such things. The way you insure your network is by protecting it. That is, treat it with tender, loving care. Remember, it took time to build the relationships that comprise it, and it took a lot of work. Don't neglect it; don't neglect the people in it. Make a deliberate effort to keep in touch with everyone on as regular a basis as *necessary*, and more importantly, make the effort to add value to their lives. When you add value to their lives, you add value to the network.

You will naturally keep in touch with some people more than others. Like all networks, yours will have an inner circle, or what Bill George refers to as "your own personal board of directors."[34] You will become so familiar with these people that regular communication is second nature. Don't take these people for granted, though, because they are the most important people in your network. As Maxwell notes, "A leader's potential is determined by the people closest to him."[35] *You* are now the leader, so choose wisely. Your inner circle is critical to your success. Additionally, give great concern to those you infrequently talk to, e-mail, or see at seminars and meetings. Go out of your way to call them, send them an e-mail, or drop a note in the mail. Invite them out for coffee or a business lunch. Reconnect with them.

Imagine networking as a dinner party where you are the host. At some point, you will need to make the rounds and greet your guests. You will spend more time talking with some guests than others, but it is imperative that you take the time to speak with *everyone*. And no matter how much time you spend with someone, you need to make that person feel as though he or she is the only one in the room, the center of all your attention. Networking is no different. You have to make your rounds on your address book on a regular basis to insure your network's value, so get out there and mingle! And remember, you aren't networking just to help yourself. Helping others by connecting them to the *right* people and *right* opportunities is money in the bank.

Using your network to benefit other people is similar to what Steve Covey refers to in *The 7 Habits of Highly Effective People* as an "Emotional Bank Account."[36] You make deposits by helping other people connect and form mutually beneficial relationships. As time passes, your bank account grows larger and allows you to make withdrawals, if necessary. The real reward is when you collect interest. That is, you get something for free because you've made a series of deposits, a dividend. A dividend in networking is when your network works for you without your direct action. It is in this manner that serving others reaps huge dividends. As Covey states, "The Emotional Bank Account is the production capability side of human relationships, human interaction."[37]

I attended a networking event at Regent University and saw several familiar faces. I ran into Matt, a gentleman with whom I graduated from business school. We chatted for a few minutes and then he told me he wanted to introduce me to someone he knew, Toks Idowu, who might be able to use someone with my experience. Toks and I stepped out into the hallway and talked for over thirty minutes. Without any effort on my part, other than serving others, I made a great connection and added someone new to my network. As it turned out, we got together later and discussed my future potential with his organization. By the way, he just so happened to be the chief executive officer of his own company! I didn't end up working for him, but we formed a lasting relationship and professional alliance that has been tremendously beneficial for both of us. We meet regularly and discuss business strategy.

Your network grows exponentially when you serve others and seek no personal gain. I've said it before, but it bears repeating, you have to give to get. By giving to others, you add value to your network and insure it for the future. As you continue to add value to the lives of others, word will spread quickly, and others will refer you and seek your advice and counsel. As I will discuss in the next chapter, networking is all about reciprocity.

Summary

Successful networks bring value to people's lives. Once you begin to add value to someone's life, you are leading. As you continue to lead, you form relationships. Some of these relationships will form your inner circle. Take the time to appraise your network. Focus on the reciprocal value of the relationships and continue to solidify them. This is the key to sustaining your network.

Think-It-Through Questions

1. Am I giving back to the people in my network?
2. Who needs to be in my network, and who doesn't?
3. Who is in my inner circle?
4. Am I making my networking rounds regularly?

Chapter Six

Sustaining the Network for the Long Haul

~Become a Servant~

I referred to the concept of *servant leadership* in the intro-
duction. As I noted, networking is about leadership,
particularly servant leadership or what I dubbed *servant
networking.*[38] Servant networking involves

> serving others and helping them achieve all they
> are capable of achieving. Servant networkers are
> leaders who think in terms of what they can do for
> other people, specifically by connecting them to
> other people. The more they give to those in their

network, the more they will receive in return and the stronger and more mutually beneficial it will become for those in it.[39]

Networking is built on relationships, and relationships involve people. Max De Pree stated, "One of the particular skills that leaders are required to exemplify in practice is the indispensible knack for building and nurturing relationships."[40]

The *New Oxford American Dictionary* defines reciprocity as "the practice of exchanging things with others for mutual benefit." Sustaining your network is based on reciprocity. "Networking requires reciprocity, and, therefore, the free-rider attitude is not ethically acceptable."[41] Ivan Misner, founder of BNI, notes four laws of reciprocity: "1. Giving means helping others achieve success. 2. The person who helps you will not necessarily be the person you helped. 3. The law of reciprocity can be measured. 4. Success takes getting involved."[42] These are excellent points and fully summarize what it means to reciprocate. They are the commandments of successful networking. When you network correctly, you do so with notion of helping others, not yourself. You may wonder how this is possible for a novice. Well, at some point you will realize you have something to offer other people and will be in a position to help them. Thus begins your journey of servant leadership. And this is what will sustain your network for the long haul.

After your network has been up and running for a while, remember to check it regularly. Just as a spider web attracts flies, networks attract people. You might just be surprised who flies into yours. For example, as part of my discharge process from the navy, I attended the Disability Transition Assistance Program (DTAP). Al Welcher, a retired senior chief petty officer, gave one of the briefs. Al runs a program called the Education and Employment Initiative (E2I). Essentially, the program places service members who are in the medical discharge pipeline in federal employment internships and provides them with practical on-the-job training in preparation for future employment. It also refers service members to local colleges and universities for training. Ideally, upon discharge, the service member will be able to walk right into a job with the federal government or complete a little training and then obtain a job. As Al informed me, E2I was connected with several of the local colleges and universities — but not Regent University.

This presented a golden opportunity for me to give back to the cornerstone of my network, Dave Boisselle. I immediately contacted him and filled him in on E2I and their connection to some of the local universities, and I provided him with Al's contact information. The connection was made. Two otherwise unconnected entities in my network were now connected. Al had unwittingly flown into my web, and the benefit gleaned was not by me directly, but by those within the network. This indirect benefit, reciprocity, is what makes networking such a powerful tool, and it is what allows you to add value to others' lives.

About six months after meeting Al and introducing him to Dave and Regent University, we all sat down with former Chief of Naval Operations (CNO) Admiral Vern Clark to discuss some of the things that were transpiring in the navy. Particularly, we spoke about unemployed veterans and E2I's role in assisting them to find jobs and get the training they need. The unemployment rate for veterans was 12.1 percent in 2011, four percent higher than for nonveterans.[43] Admiral Clark listened as Al, Dave, and I provided our piece of the puzzle about the level of unemployed veterans and what we could do to provide training to help them find jobs. He shared his experience and perspective with us about how to proceed on both a macro and micro level. Networking provided the opportunity for three former enlisted sailors to sit with the former CNO and have a meaningful and relevant conversation *to impact the lives of others!*

The reciprocation was not over, though. Al had been working to bring E2I to some of the local commands. With me, he had an inside man at his command. Not only was I senior in rank, I was also in the medical discharge process. I knew the turf and was able to connect Al with other person-nel in the same predicament. Al was able to bring E2I to the command, which benefitted many service members and allowed the command to share responsibility for their continued well-being and future career success outside the military. And when service members benefit, the military benefits and society benefits.

In addition to working with the command, Al took the time to work with my referrals. I frequently referred sailors to Al, and he worked with all of them. He provided guidance in resume and cover letter preparation, taught them interview techniques, and conducted mock interviews. He also put them in touch with representatives from the Veteran's Association and Physical Evaluation Board office. People I referred benefited from Al's invaluable expertise and dedication to make a difference in the lives of service members. That's the value of networking!

One person flew into my network. I was able to connect that person to several people within the network and add value to their lives, value that will have a lasting impact. And when it was time for reciprocation, Al was more than ready to share the wealth with others in the network. Sharing the wealth is the only way to sustain your network for the long haul. The more you share, the wealthier you become.

~Share the Wealth~

In the process of writing this book, Dave Boisselle asked me to speak to Regent University's Student Veterans Association about my experience and how networking was positively impacting my ability to find a job. At the luncheon, I met Sam, a young man in his twenties who had just finished joint master's degrees in government and divinity. He was in the army reserves awaiting selection to the chaplain corps. Sam and I spoke after the luncheon for a bit. He later contacted me and asked if we could meet to further discuss networking techniques, particularly as they pertained to his situation. Of course, I agreed.

We got together and had a great discussion. We remained in contact via e-mail and still do today. One day I received an e-mail from a colleague of Sam's, Rick. Sam had taken the initiative and apprised him of my pending discharge from the navy and asked if he could possibly help me in my search for a job. This was a bona fide dividend and is what networking is all about. Without my prompting, Sam not only offered to help me, he *reciprocated*! And by reciprocating, he brought someone new into the network. The spider web grew a little bigger. More importantly, though, Sam was practicing servant networking. When you take the time to genuinely care about others and work to positively impact someone's life without seeking personal gain, you reap the greatest rewards from networking.

One story comes to mind about the expansive nature of reciprocity. It's not limited to giving back to only those you know or with whom you network. One of the counselors who assisted me during my transition process contacted me and asked whether I could help her son. He had been having a tough time finding a job. One of the key issues he had was he didn't have much experience. He did have a very good education, though. I looked at his resume and made some suggestions to improve it based on my experience dealing with hiring authorities and headhunting firms. As fate would have it, a colleague posted an advertisement for a friend of his who provide resume service as well as job search strategy counseling. I was able to help this young man by connecting him to someone I didn't even know. In the process, I helped two people and added someone to my network, and it was all due to reciprocity.

Reciprocity is what distinguishes *servant networking* from just networking. In discussing networking, Mele stated, "The strength of a relationship between two persons is related to the frequency, reciprocity, emotional intensity, and intimacy of the relationship."[44] Make no mistake about it; networking is about forming relationships.

As you continue to share the wealth with others, your network will expand. Along the way, though, some relationships will require mending. Perhaps you lost contact with someone or forgot to return a phone call or e-mail. Or maybe you had a minor disagreement with someone over something petty. These things happen even in the best of networks, but fortunately they can be repaired. Pick up the phone, send an e-mail, or better yet meet face-to-face. As Warhoe notes, "The purest form of networking is face-to-face, whether it is a lunch meeting during the work week or attending a large conference with thousands of attendees, and meeting new contacts or reconnecting with old friends and colleagues."[45] No matter how successful you become at networking, you must remember to add the personal touch of face-to-face communications on a regular basis. This enables you to keep your relationships current, and keeping your relationships current affords you the opportunity to know the needs of those in your network and provides the opportunity to reciprocate.

Reciprocity is the foundation of relationships. They are built on trust and respect. A survey in the *Internal Journal of Business and Management* noted, "It was revealed that face-to-face communication has more comprehensive impact in terms of facilitating the interpersonal trust building mechanisms."[46] While e-mail, text messages, and correspondence have their place, nothing surpasses face-to-face communication for effectiveness and meaning. And by engaging in face-to-face communication on a regular basis, those in our network can learn our strengths and we theirs. As Stephen Warhoe stated so precisely in *The Value of Networking*, "Those who know you must also know about your strengths and the areas at which you excel. Otherwise, how will those in our network market us?"[47] Indeed. How will we know how to market them and in turn reciprocate? Get out there and meet face-to-face!

Continue to give to others and add value to your network. By doing so, your network will increase in size and value. Meet in person on a regular basis, assess the needs of those in your network, and reciprocate. Doing so will sustain your network for the long haul.

Summary

Sustaining your network involves reciprocity. The more you give, the more you will receive, and the more value your network will have. Meet face-to-face on a regular basis, mend relationships, and catch up with your colleagues. Continuing to build trusting relationships will sustain your network.

Think-It-Through Questions

1. Who in my network needs help?
2. Am I meeting face-to-face with those in my network regularly?
3. How can I serve my network?

AFTERWORD

T he phrase "you only get out of it what you put into it" is true for networking. If you don't make any effort to get to know people and attempt to reciprocate, you won't benefit from networking. Networking takes time and more energy than most people imagine. But when done correctly, it is one of the most rewarding experiences you will ever have because it not only allows you to grow, it allows you to impact others' lives in a positive way. And that's something that just can't be equaled.

Networking is not only the back door into a job or your own business, but the front door into exclusive relationships. While others are busy pounding the pavement and filling out applications, you can be engaging in conversations with the people who have the final say on who gets hired or who receives financing for their business venture. Your ability to mingle and influence others will take you on a journey that will shape your life and career as well as land you the job of your dreams, whether it's with an employer or your own enterprise. You will meet more people and make more connections than you ever thought possible, and it all begins with a smile and saying, "Hello." More importantly, though, every conversation should end with, "What can I do for you?"

Serving your network and those in it is the key component to becoming a successful networker. And as with all service, it takes time, initiative, tremendous effort, dedication, and sacrifice. I've often said *work* is the four-letter word that makes networking successful. There is more than a grain of truth in that statement. I spend many hours each week maintaining contact with those in my various networks. Over time, I've added many people to my networks, which has increased the amount of time necessary to maintain the relationships. Even though it keeps me very busy, serving my network—connecting others and witnessing the benefits—is one of the most rewarding activities in my life.

You can't build a network overnight, but you can take the first step toward doing so. Engage others in conversation, ascertain their needs, and meet face-to-face frequently. Realize *you* have something of value to offer and give it freely. You'll be surprised how effective a networker you will become. Networking is a journey that will transform your life and inspire others to do the same.

Recommended Reading and Resources

Carnegie, Dale (1936). *How to Win Friends and Influence People*. New York, NY: Simon & Schuster.

George, Bill (2007). *True North*. San Francisco, CA: Jossey-Bass.

Gladwell, Malcolm (2002). *The Tipping Point*. New York, NY: Back Bay Books.

Keller, Jeff (1999). *Attitude Is Everything*. East Norwich, NY: Attitude Is Everything, Inc. Publishing.

Mackay, Harvey (1997). Dig *Your Well before You're Thirsty: The Only Networking Book You'll Ever Need*. New York, NY: Doubleday.

Maxwell, John (2007). *The 21 Irrefutable Laws of Leadership*. Nashville, TN: Thomas Nelson, Inc.

RoAne, Susan (1993). *The Secrets of Savvy Networking: How to Make the Best Connections for Business and Personal Success*. New York, NY: Warner Books, Inc.

———(2000). *How to Work a Room*. New York, NY: Harper Collins.

NOTES

[1] RoAne, S. (n.d.). *Create a Network of Colleagues, Cronies, Clients and Friends*. Retrieved from: www.susanroane.com/articles/connect.html.

[2] Maxwell, J. (2007). *The Twenty-One Irrefutable Laws of Leadership*. Nashville, TN: Thomas Nelson, Inc.

[3] Bradley, S. (2007). *How to influence your network*. Retrieved from: www.networkingeffectively.com/?p=27.

[4] Latour, M. (2004). *Dynamic Followership: The Prerequisite for Effective Leadership*. Retrieved from: www.airpower.maxwell.af.mil/airchronicles/apj/apj04/win04/latour.html.

[5] Spears, L. (2002). *Focus on Leadership: Servant Leadership for the Twenty-First Century*. Retrieved from: Google books, page 13.

[6] Shearer, D. P. (2009). *In You God Trusts*. Xulon Press.

[7] Fallows, S., & Steven, C. (2000). Building employability skills into the higher education curriculum: A university-wide initiative. *Education & Training, 42*(2), 75–83. http://0-search.proquest.com.library.regent.edu/docview/237066619?accountid=13479.

[8] Chartrand, S. (1997). *Employers Devise New Strategies to Test Job Applicants*. Retrieved from: http://partners.nytimes.com/library/jobmarket/121497sabra.html.

[9] RoAne, S. (n.d.) *Networking: Beyond the Buzzword*. Retrieved from: www.susanroane.com/articles/beyond-buzzword.html.

[10] Ibarra, H. & Hunter, M. (2007). *How Leaders Create and Use Networks*. Retrieved from: http://hbr.org/2007/01/how-leaders-create-and-use-networks/ar/1.

[11] Melé, D. (2009). The practice of networking: An ethical approach. *Journal of Business Ethics, 90,* 487–503. doi:10.1007/s10551-010-0602-2.

[12] Keller, J. *Attitude Is Everything*. East Norwich, NY: Attitude Is Everything, Inc. Publishing.

[13] Pappano, L. (2011). *The Masters as the New Bachelors*. Retrieved from: www.nytimes.com/2011/07/24/education/edlife/edl-24masters-t.html?pagewanted=all.

[14] Hopkins, K. (2012). *Best Value College: U.S. News and World Report*. Retrieved from: www.huffingtonpost.com/2012/09/13/best-value-colleges-us-ne_n_1880275.html.

[15] Gladwell, M. (2010). *The Tipping Point*. New York, NY: Back Bay Books.

[16] Fisher, A. (2008). *Be a Better Networker*. Retrieved from: http://money.cnn.com/2008/11/06/news/economy/networking.fortune/index.htm.

[17] Maxwell, J. (2007). *The Twenty-One Irrefutable Laws of Leadership*. Nashville, TN: Thomas Nelson, Inc.

[18] *A Suitable Wardrobe*. (2007). Retrieved from: http://asuitablewardrobe.dynend.com/2007_01_01_archive.html.

[19] Carnegie, D. (1936). How to Win Friends and Influence People. New York, NY: Simon & Schuster.

[20] Gladwell, M. (2002). *The Tipping Point*. New York, NY: Back Bay Books.

[21] Maxwell, J. (2011). Executive Leadership Series. Virginia Beach, VA: Regent University.

[22] Carnegie, D. (1936). *How to Win Friends and Influence People*. New York, NY: Simon & Schuster.

[23] Gladwell, M. (2002). *The Tipping Point*. New York, NY: Back Bay Books.

[24] Misner, I. (2009). *You Never Know Whom They Know*. Retrieved from: www.entrepreneur.com/article/199542.

[25] Carnegie, D. (1936). *How to Win Friends and Influence People*. New York, NY: Simon & Schuster.

[26] Misner, I. (2007). *The Key to Networking*. Retrieved from: www.entrepreneur.com/article/175158.

[27] Carnegie, D. (1936). *How to Win Friends and Influence People*. New York, NY: Simon & Schuster.

[28] Kennedy, J. (1961). Inaugural Address. Retrieved from http://www.ushistory.org/documents/ask-not.htm

[29] Producer, Frankish, B. E. , & Director, Robinson, P. A. (1989). Field of Dreams. United States: Universal Pictures.

[30] Gladwell, M. (2002). *The Tipping Point*. New York, NY: Back Bay Books.

[31] *De Beers*. (n.d.). Retrieved from: http://en.wikipedia.org/wiki/De_Beers.

[32] RoAne, S. (n.d.) *Networking: Beyond the Buzzword*. Retrieved from: www.susanroane.com/articles/beyond-buzzword.html.

[33] Maxwell, J. (2007). *The Twenty-One Irrefutable Laws of Leadership*. Nashville, TN: Thomas Nelson, Inc.

[34] George, B. (2007). *True North*. San Francisco, CA: Jossey-Bass.

[35] Ibid.

[36] Covey, S. (2004). *The Seven Habits of Highly Effective People*. Retrieved from: Google Books.

[37] Ibid.

[38] Bishop, W. (2011). Servant networking: Leading and connecting through service. *Leadership Advance Online, XXI*. Retrieved from: www.regent.edu/acad/global/publications/lao.

[39] Ibid.

[40] De Pree, M. (1987). *The Art of Leadership*. New York, NY: Doubleday.

[41] Melé, D. (2009). The practice of networking: An ethical approach. *Journal of Business Ethics, 90*, 487–503. doi:10.1007/s10551-010-0602-2

[42] Misner, I. (2010). *Learning to Use the Law of Reciprocity: 4 Tips*. Retrieved from: http://businessnetworking.com/learning-to-use-the-law-of-reciprocity%E2%80%93four-tips.

[43] Kurtzleben, D. (2012). *Iraq and Afghanistan Vets Saw High Unemployment in 2011*. Retrieved from: www.usnews.com/news/articles/2012/03/20/iraq-and-afghanistan-vets-saw-high-unemployment-in-2011.

[44] Melé, D. (2009). The practice of networking: An ethical approach. *Journal of Business Ethics, 90*, 487–503. doi:10.1007/s10551-010-0602-2.

[45] Warhoe, Stephen P, PE,C.C.E., C.F.C.C. (2008). The value of networking. *Cost Engineering, 50*(10), 3–4. http://0-search.proquest.com.library. regent.edu/docview/220447404?accountid=13479.

[46] Zeffane, R., Tipu, S.A., & Ryan, J. C. (2011). Communication, commitment & trust: Exploring the triad. *International Journal of Business and Management, 6*(6), 77–87. http://0-search.proquest.com.library.regent. edu/docview/872115710?accountid=13479.

[47] Warhoe, Stephen P, PE,C.C.E., C.F.C.C. (2008). The value of networking. *Cost Engineering, 50*(10), 3–4. http://0-search.proquest.com.library. regent.edu/docview/220447404?accountid=13479.

William Bishop is the chief executive officer and founder of the Bishop Advisory Group, LLC, a consulting company that harnesses the power of critical thinking to provide practical solutions. He is a veteran of the United States Navy, where he ascended to the rank of chief petty officer in seven years. During his naval service, he successfully formed, trained, coached, and led integrated, cross-functional teams across a variety of platforms and combat situations to achieve complex mission objectives. He served as a leadership facilitator and later as a program manager for one of the navy's three enlisted leadership programs at the Center for Naval Leadership (CNL), where he designed, developed, and revised the navy's enlisted leadership curriculum. His dynamic and energetic style made him a highly sought and engaging facilitator. The contributions he made to CNL had a lasting impact navy-wide, and many of his ideas and designs are still in use today.

Bill is now a doctoral student at Regent University, where he pioneered and promulgated the concept of servant networking. He is also a prolific author whose works have been featured in Talent Management magazine, the Journal of Strategic Leadership, Proceedings magazine, the Journal of Values-Based Leadership, and Leadership Advance Online. Going Home: A Troop's Guide to Successfully

Transitioning to the Real World is his first book. He holds degrees from Excelsior College (BS), Regent University (MBA), and is a graduate of Harvard Business School's Executive Education Program (Authentic Leadership Development).